A FIRST CLASS TOWNSHIP

A First Class Township

Jack Swersie

authorHOUSE®

AuthorHouse™ LLC
1663 Liberty Drive
Bloomington, IN 47403
www.authorhouse.com
Phone: 1-800-839-8640

Published by AuthorHouse   03/14/2014

ISBN: 978-1-4918-6330-5 (sc)
ISBN: 978-1-4918-6331-2 (e)

Library of Congress Control Number: 2014902737

Any people depicted in stock imagery provided by Thinkstock are models,
and such images are being used for illustrative purposes only.
Certain stock imagery © Thinkstock.

This book is printed on acid-free paper.

Because of the dynamic nature of the Internet, any web addresses or links contained
in this book may have changed since publication and may no longer be valid. The views
expressed in this work are solely those of the author and do not necessarily reflect the
views of the publisher, and the publisher hereby disclaims any responsibility for them.

Contents

About The Author

Born and raised on Long Island, New York, Jack Swersie has been a Pocono Township resident for over 26 years. Leaving New York in 1971, Swersie then lived in Michigan, Georgia, Louisiana and North Carolina before settling in Scotrun, Pennsylvania in 1987.

As a professional comedy entertainer for 35 years, he has shared the stage with some of the most legendary performers of the 20th century and chronicles his career in his published eBook *Opening Act* available at Amazon.com.

Swersie became involved in Pocono Township issues in 2006 and joined forces with Pocono First Initiative in 2013. His participation with the group and its ultimate outcome have brought him a level of satisfaction and pride that no other personal endeavor ever has, and it is that sense of accomplishment which has inspired him to write this account of the yearlong effort.

It is his hope that this historical recollection will serve as not only a blueprint, but as an inspiration for others looking to change their local governance for the better.

Acknowledgments

My written account of the Pocono First Initiative is dedicated to the ensemble of residents who selflessly gave their time, money and hard work to make a positive difference for everyone in Pocono Township. This unlikely alliance of diverse individuals, along with those who voted to support the referendum, deserves much praise and many thanks.

Kudos to my new friends for life: Judi Coover, Monica Gerrity, Bob Demarest, Shirley Demarest, Richard Wielebinski, Debra Morrishow, Diane Zweifel, Donald Simpson, Scott Gilliland, Jake Singer, John Bramley, Taylor Munoz, Linda Kresge, Marie Guidry, Maxine Turbolski, Ruth Perfetti, Roger Hanna, Roy Smith and Linda Smith.

Special thanks to Judi Coover for her inspiring leadership. She was the guiding force behind Pocono First. Without her, the status-quo would today reign supreme in our community.

Thanks to Judi Coover, Debra Morrishow and Bill Below for fact-checking and proof-reading my original manuscript.

My sincere gratitude also goes out to Pocono Record staff writer David Pierce. His exacting coverage of local issues provided clear and convincing evidence of the need for change and allowed residents to make a well-informed decision regarding the future of Pocono Township.

Jack Swersie

It was never political. Nor was it personal. It was simply a matter of right or wrong. And in early 2013, many residents felt that something was wrong with the way Pocono Township was governed.

Located in the heart of the Pocono Mountains in Northeast Pennsylvania, Pocono Township, comprising 35 square miles, was created as a separate township by a decree of the courts of Northampton County in November, 1816. In 1830 the population was 564,[1] growing to over 11,000 residents by 2013.

Since its creation, Pocono Township was a township of the second class. In fact, most Pennsylvania townships are of the second class. According to the 1933 Pennsylvania Second Class Township Code, townships throughout the commonwealth are divided into classes; townships of the first class, townships of the second class or home rule townships. All townships that are not townships of the first class or home rule townships are townships of the second class.[2]

Second class townships in Pennsylvania are governed by a board of three or five elected supervisors (BOS), each serving a six-year term. They are paid a small fee for attending meetings which is determined by law, based on population. With 11,000 residents, Pocono Township supervisors were compensated $3,250/year. Supervisors are entitled to township health benefits and, if they are holding a paid township job, they are also entitled to be part of the township pension plan.

---

[1]   Pocono Township Website: http://www.poconotownship.org/township/
[2]   PSATS Website, Second Class Code: http://www.psats.org/subpage.php?pageid=secondclasstownshipcode#II

Supervisors are allowed to appoint themselves to paid township jobs such as road master, secretary, treasurer, assistant secretary and/or assistant treasurer. Salaries for those jobs are set by a board of elected auditors.

In 2013, our BOS included Harold Werkheiser, Frank Hess and the newest member, Henry Bengel. Hess served as chairman, after the retirement of Supervisor Chairwoman Jane Cilurso.

CHAPTER 2
"THE TOWNSHIP IS GOING TO FALL APART"

My involvement with the township began in 2006 when long-time supervisor Pat Ross was at the helm. My dear friend, the late-Edward Elliott, who once sat on the township Planning Commission and later held the job of Zoning Enforcement Officer, had been going to BOS meetings for almost two decades and I joined him one Monday night. It wasn't a particularly interesting meeting and I would continue attending only on occasion for the next four or five years.

In 2011, Jane Cilurso chaired the BOS and Frank Hess was relatively new on the board. Harold Werkheiser had been on the job since 2008 after running against Pat Ross and winning the election by a small number of votes.

A bridge near my home had collapsed and the township didn't have money in their budget to repair it. When supervisors started discussing the hiring of a township manager, I thought it contradictory that they would have enough money for a new position, but not to repair the bridge. I already had a letter to the editor about this matter published in our local newspaper, the Pocono Record, when I went to a meeting and made a public comment about my concern.

My comment, along with those of many other residents, was duly noted. Under Cilurso's leadership, when residents spoke up, the BOS listened and a township manager was never hired while she was chairwoman. In time, the bridge was repaired.

What I witnessed at that meeting fueled my interest in attending more often. There was a troubling divide between the supervisors. A two-to-one dynamic was keeping Hess out of the loop and there was seething anger between him and the other two. Hess had many supporters at the Monday night meetings who didn't like seeing him marginalized and they were quite vocal. An unsettling tension filled the room. It wasn't a healthy environment for effective governing and clearly wasn't beneficial to the taxpayers of Pocono Township. I found it all very disturbing and wanted to keep an eye on it. So, I did.

Jane Cilurso was soon to retire and many, including myself, looked forward to the possibility of Hess taking over as chairman once she departed. It was widely believed that he'd do a great job once unfettered.

I vigorously argued with my dear friend Ed Elliott when he told me that *"the township is going to fall apart"* when Cilurso leaves.

I didn't realize at the time, but Ed's words could not have been closer to the truth!

Former New York policeman, Henry Bengel, was working as an advertising executive for the Pocono Record when he campaigned to fill the vacancy left by Jane Cilurso's retirement. He ran as a write-in candidate against small-business owner and volunteer fireman Donald Simpson. Financially backed by a cabal of local business owners known as Concerned Citizens of Pocono Township (CCPT), Bengel ran in part promising not to seek a paid township job should he win the election.

And win he did! Simpson's calm and confident demeanor and solid history of local volunteerism was no match for the more animated Bengel aura. One cannot underestimate the effect that thousands of dollars donated by CCPT had on the election outcome. When it comes to campaign donations, local politics is no different than national.

As politics will have it, campaign promises fade and a year later a most brazen move would be made by Frank Hess and Henry Bengel. It happened at the annual township reorganization meeting on January 7th, 2013.

Reorganization meetings are held once a year, the express purpose of such meetings being to appoint township officers. That night, following over a dozen appointments including solicitor, engineer, zoning officer, police chief, assistant police chief, and sewage enforcement officer, supervisor Harold Werkheiser made a motion to reappoint himself to the position of road master, a job he had already held for a number of years. A deafening silence followed. Neither Hess nor Bengel would second the motion.

Hess then made a motion to nominate Bengel to the road master position and that was quickly seconded by Bengel himself. Both supervisors tried to immediately vote on the nomination but there was an uproar by those in attendance at the meeting. Loud and angry public comment followed, but to no avail. Ignoring the will of the people, the supervisors voted on the motion anyway. Hess and Bengel voted Bengel into the road master position. It appeared that a deal had previously been brokered between the two majority supervisors to appoint Bengel to the road master position.

The Pennsylvania Sunshine Act states that "the General Assembly hereby declares it to be the public policy of this Commonwealth to insure the right of its citizens to have notice of and the right to attend all meetings of agencies at which any agency business is discussed or acted upon."[3]

By Hess and Bengel meeting behind closed doors to privately discuss the removal of Werkheiser as road master and the appointment of Bengel, the question would be raised as to whether they had violated the spirit of the Sunshine Act.

This move on the part of the two supervisors was made despite Bengel's total lack of related work experience and his campaign promise not to take a paid township job. To further offend the sensibilities of residents, Bengel requested a $72,000/year salary!

Defending his action, he said that when he made his 2011 campaign promise, he could only rely on what he knew at the time. Over the last year, however, he said things changed. *"I was basing that on information I had at the time,"* he said. *"I didn't lie to anybody. When I got into office, I saw a need that needed to be fulfilled."*[4]

Residents were outraged. Harold Werkheiser had lived in Pocono Township all of his life and worked for the township long before he became supervisor. No one could deny he ran a stellar road department. Public antagonism toward the two supervisors grew as Bengel ignored the will of those who voted him into

---

3   Pennsylvania Sunshine Act: http://webpages.charter.net/gdsbmmllp/sunshine.htm

4   Sadowski, M., "Things change for Pocono Supervisor Bengel" Pocono Record (1/9/13) http://www.poconorecord.com/apps/pbcs.dll/article?AID=/20130109/NEWS/301090327/0/NEWS040301

office and steadfastly refused to right his wrong by stepping down.

On January 23rd, 2013, the Pocono Record published a letter to the editor which I wrote, objecting to their actions, while trying to remain diplomatic.

Bengel should step aside as road master
In Your Opinion—Pocono Record

There has been a groundswell of anger and resentment aimed toward Pocono Township's newest supervisor, Henry Bengel, because of his recent decision to vote himself into the $72,000-per-year position as road master. This move was made despite his lack of related experience and his campaign promise not to do so.

It is my opinion, as well as the opinion of others in the township, that he should reconsider this decision, step aside, and with the assistance of the other supervisors, seek out and hire someone with the proper experience at a salary commensurate with that experience.

If Mr. Bengel is to continue to perform the good job that he has up to now been doing, it is imperative for him to maintain the respect and admiration he has rightfully earned since being voted into his position of township supervisor. And the only way I believe he can do that is to reverse what many in the community, including myself, believe to be wrong.[5]—**Jack Swersie**

Months later, after many other highly critical letters and pointed articles in the Pocono Record and heated discourse at the township meetings (one particularly unfortunate episode involving his supportive family members in attendance), Bengel

---

[5] Swersie, J., "Bengel should step aside as road master" In Your Opinion, Pocono Record (1/23/13), http://www.poconorecord.com/apps/pbcs.dll/article?AID=/20130123/NEWS04/301230305/-1/NEWSMAP

could bear the public scorn no more and relinquished the road master job. Still, he and Hess refused to reappoint Werkheiser.

The damage inflicted upon their reputations as elected officials and the problems created for the township were great. Not only was public trust toward Hess and Bengel damaged, a lawsuit was filed against the township by Werkheiser. This understandable legal action on the part of Werkheiser could potentially cost the township thousands of dollars in litigation fees and more should the defendants lose.

The removal of Werkheiser as road master and the subsequent lawsuit was a turning point for many residents, including me. I knew things had not been running smoothly under the current BOS, but I was timid about getting involved. I had known Frank Hess since the late 1980s and had a great amount of respect for him. I liked him. He's a self-made man and a delightful guy. He started F/J Hess & Sons Plumbing & Heating about the same time I bought my home and over the years he grew his business into a hugely successful operation, providing "a comprehensive range of products and services to nearly 14,000 satisfied individuals and businesses"[6] in the Poconos. His business acumen earned him well-deserved recognition and admiration in the Poconos and surely helped him win his supervisor seat in 2009.

Still, I was deeply troubled by the way he and Bengel mistreated Werkheiser. They effectively took this man's livelihood for the simple reason that Bengel decided he wanted that job. You just don't treat people the way they treated Werkheiser. It was wrong, plain and simple. I could no longer support leaders who could be so indifferent to others.

I wanted change.

---

[6]   F/J Hess & Sons Website: http://www.fjhess.com/

CHAPTER 4
CONCERNED CITIZENS

Who are the Concerned Citizens of Pocono Township?

This group of local developers, business owners and their friends had worked quietly over the past couple of years to gain influence over the BOS and already had the ears of two out of the three supervisors. With Werkheiser's six-year term soon to end, it was likely they would try for a third. The prevailing sentiment among many residents-in-the-know was that a number of CCPT members were concerned about one thing and one thing only—control.

I am not going to mention individual names of those associated with the group. Who they are is not important. They are not public figures and they are not necessarily bad people. In fact, if you look at the big picture, in the end, folks like these create jobs and build the economy of the communities where they develop their businesses. That is admirable.

While some of these individuals may be motivated by the need to feel in control, others say they simply want to see "pro-business" people running their local government.

Because they have the financial means, they are able to select and support candidates favorable to their own business interests, with the hope of gaining control and influence over a majority of the local leadership.

It shouldn't be that way. It doesn't even have to be. In fact, there are many other developers and business owners who achieve the same level of success without having to feel as though they must have undue influence over their elected leaders.

But that is the way it is.

Small town politics in America!

Anyone regularly attending BOS meetings would have been impressed by Judi Coover. Nobody was more of a treasure trove of knowledge and more vocal when it came to township issues. Her suggestions to the BOS were many and her warranted critiques were always direct and eloquently stated. She was among the smartest in the room. Supervisors appeared to like her but if they didn't, they never really showed it. They could never deny that this retired technology lawyer and long-time township resident knew her stuff. She arrived at every meeting armed with a firm understanding of any subject she planned on addressing. Never was she shy expressing her views nor was she ever intimidated when it came to challenging the local power elite.

"Good government is a gift from God!" she says. She firmly believes that government has a good and proper role, has grown outside its boundaries while amassing excessive power and has fallen prey to extensive corruption. She further believes that the only way to fix it is at the local level. *"I felt the need to try and become part of an effort to right the role of government at its most local and in some ways, most significant level."* She believes that this can only happen by *"either changing the hearts of those in power or exchanging those in power with those who believe in good and fair government."*

Like any astute observer of local issues, Judi was more than aware that there were serious deficiencies within our BOS. It concerned her that the board was habitually unprepared for their meetings. There was no planning for future township growth. Protocol wasn't being followed. Public workshops were abolished. A township administrator was hired without the required vote and ordinance, and without a contract or job description. Job descriptions which the township paid to have written were not being used for any of the township positions, including those jobs held by supervisors. Time clocks were purchased in an effort to curb excessive overtime pay but never utilized by the police department for which they were purchased. The board interviewed applicants for the road master position made vacant by their ill-advised firing of Werkheiser but refused to fill the position.

It was clear to Judi that the supervisors were ignoring the will of the people. According to her, the tipping point was "*the repeated tin ear of the supervisors, meeting after meeting, as we pleaded with them to reconsider their actions with Werkheiser. It became clear that they did not work for us.*"

Enough was enough! It was time for action.

CHAPTER 6

A GRASSROOTS MOVEMENT IS BORN

I received an email from Judi asking if I would be interested in attending a meeting at her home. She had assembled a small group of informed residents to discuss options available for improving the governance of our township. Somewhat reluctant at first, I ultimately accepted the invitation. I'm glad I did.

What was to follow would be an unparalleled grassroots effort to make a difference at the local level. Under Judi's focused leadership and against strong odds, our nonpartisan team of selfless, intelligent, hard-working and dedicated residents set out to find a better way forward in Pocono Township.

We met on a cold and snowy evening in early March, 2013. In attendance were a fascinating group of individuals, soon to form an unlikely alliance.

Monica Gerrity saw too much wrong in the way Pocono Township was being governed and knew that it was time to act. Never afraid of standing up to those in power, this bright, articulate and outspoken young lady always had an impressive command of the issues of which she spoke. And, like Judi, she was usually right.

Born in Pocono Township and raised by politically active parents, Monica learned at an early age that she should always fight for what was right, whether it was popular sentiment or not. In 2005, acting as a spokesperson for neighboring property owners, she vehemently fought against one resident's request to change all of their zoning from residential to commercial. Asserting that such rezoning would negatively affect the investments made in their homes and their quality of life[7], she won her battle and that encouraged her continued involvement in local matters.

From then on, *"When certain issues would come up that I felt would negatively affect the town, if I thought that by being involved I could somehow change it, I would take a stand."*

In 2013, there were many problems within the BOS that were adversely affecting Pocono Township and Monica was fearless in confronting the supervisors on those matters. But she felt as though they weren't listening, didn't care and never would. Once again, she knew It was time to take a stand.

Retired psychiatric social worker Diane Zweifel lived in Pocono Township since the 1970s and, after attending BOS meetings for a few years, had reached her wit's end. This sharp, well-educated and confident University of Connecticut alumnus was convinced the majority supervisors cared little about the concerns of our residents. She was equally disturbed by the degree of favoritism we were seeing between the supervisors and certain members of CCPT. She says she became involved in large part because she was *"concerned about how things were handled by the BOS regarding the average citizen who was not part of the power elite."*

If anyone was as close to being an encyclopedia of knowledge as Judi, it was 24-year-old Taylor Munoz, the youngest member of what was soon to become a seamlessly-managed and highly-determined team.

Born in the Pocono Mountains and a resident of Pocono Township for 18 years, Taylor was home-schooled by his parents and went on to earn a degree in Business Administration with a minor in Political Science at Messiah College in Grantham, Pennsylvania.

Smart and self-assured, humble and charismatic, Taylor's demeanor projected an air of confidence of someone twice his

---

7   Grape-Garvey, C., "Henryville supers to view zoning bid" Pocono Record (11/28/05) http://www.poconorecord.com/apps/pbcs.dll/article?AID=/20051128/NEWS/311289996&cid=sitesearch

age. As Government Affairs Director of a local trade association and a member of the Pocono Township Planning Commission, he already had a lot on his plate when he sat down at the table with the group. His participation would prove to be indispensable to our efforts.

Taylor strongly believed in good governance and, after witnessing the ongoing conflicts within our BOS, believed that there must be a better way forward. It wasn't personal. He liked the supervisors. He just wanted to *"modernize the way the township functions"* and *"ensure the right governing framework, so as to bring added transparency"* to our leadership.

As a member of the planning board, he saw *"little willingness to work with the Planning Commission"* on the part of the BOS and that was troubling to him. The Planning Commission was supposed to be an advisory board and they were not just being sidelined, they were being completely ignored.

Taylor, like many others, believed that it was time to research options and take necessary steps to improve our local government.

In fact, a total of four of our seven township Planning Commissioners saw the same need for change and became part of the team. Robert (Bob) Demarest had been on the commission for thirty years, twelve of them as chairman. He says that the commission had always been supportive of business development but he had tired of seeing the *"bending, stretching and breaking"* of regulations by those with influence seeking permits. On top of that, variances to zoning regulations were being given to a connected few without them having to prove hardship, which is required by code. The general consensus among Planning Commissioners was that the BOS were not including them in the township planning process, and that was summed up in a letter in the Pocono Record written by Bob.

Involve local planners in road improvements
In Your Opinion—Pocono Record

I read with interest Sunday's Pocono Record article in the business section, "Improvements to Tannersville interchange are slowly coming," and wondered why, as a member of Pocono Township's Planning Commission, I have heard so little about what is being proposed as "improvements to our road system." I've asked many times in the past few years when we as "local planners" would be included in the process spoken of in this article. When our local Pocono Township residents ask what I know about this plan, I must respond that we know nothing because we planners have not been permitted to be involved.[8]—**Bob Demarest**

Scott Gilliland's involvement in the township began in 2010 when he was appointed to the Planning Commission. Having just retired from public service after 34 years as a teacher, principal and central office administrator, he was eager to give back to the community and put to use his years of administrative and facility management experience.

Scott had voted in every election since he moved to Swiftwater, Pennsylvania in 1980, but never considered himself to be politically active. He never attended township meetings except when directed to do so as a representative of the Planning Commission. All that changed with the firing of Werkheiser. While that deeply troubled him, there were a host of other concerns that drove him to regularly attended BOS meetings.

"I observed supervisors making many ill-advised decisions; some which I felt were the result of undue influence by local business leaders. I observed an unwillingness to bring our township zoning regulations up to date or to honestly seek public input on

---

[8]   Demarest, R., "Involve local planners in road improvements" In Your Opinion, Pocono Record (12/1/13) http://www.poconorecord.com/apps/pbcs.dll/article?AID=/20131201/NEWS04/312010314/-1/NEWS0401

any issue. In two years they had not remotely planned for future initiatives. Additionally they had no working understanding of how to develop a budget or how to implement one. Their inept fiscal management lowered taxes while township assets were not adequately maintained. Road improvements and capital equipment purchases were almost non-existent under this administration. Their leadership lacked substance as well as a viable vision to move our township forward. As a result I concluded that we had a township that was run by two individuals with very limited experience who were totally ineffective in carrying out the mission of the township."

Reflecting on his time on the Planning Commission he recalled, "I felt a total lack of support for the group's efforts by two of the supervisors as well as an extreme lack of respect for commission members. I always had the impression that they just went through the motions and that their decisions were based on preconceived notions and political alliances and not on actual facts and recommendations that were presented to them."

Those realities led Scott to conclude that Pocono Township needed to change its leadership and its form of governance. Scott would become an invaluable addition to the newly formed group.

Bloomsburg University graduate Marie Guidry earned her B.A. in Elementary Education in 1978, a B.S. in Geology in 1981 and later still became a Certified Public Accountant. After working for ten years as Senior Accountant for a Stroudsburg, Pennsylvania accounting firm, she spent another nine years working for the East Stroudsburg School District as Supervisor of Financial Affairs and later as Business Manager. In 2011 she retired from the Easton Area School District in Easton, Pennsylvania after serving three years as their Business Manager. Since retirement she had been busy volunteering for the Monroe County Historical Association, the Monroe County Archives, and the Pocono Jackson Historical Society.

Marie had been going to township meetings for a number of years before becoming a member of the planning board. She viewed the interaction between the BOS and the Planning

Commission the same way as Taylor, Bob and Scott and was also disturbed by the situation between Hess, Bengel and Werkheiser.

The idea that the BOS were employing a township administrator without the required publicly adopted ordinance bothered her as well. *"Two of the current supervisors seem to have a great deal of difficulty understanding that they are required to govern in public. The requirement to conduct business in public is to protect the taxpayer's interests. Why is this so difficult for supervisors Frank Hess and Henry Bengel? Have they forgotten whom they serve?"*[9]

Shirley Demarest had never before been involved in day-to-day township matters but instead volunteered her time working with the Meesing Nature Center and the Nature Conservancy, as well as the Pocono/Jackson Historical Society.

Born in Barbados, moving to the United States in 1950 and now holding dual citizenship, this former registered nurse considers herself a very proud American.

After attending township meetings with the current board she became disillusioned. *"Having been exposed to American democracy, I have of late been made aware of a gradual erosion of the wonderful democratic process in our local government. And after 53-years living in Pocono Township with my husband Bob, I've seen many changes; some good and some not productive for all of our citizens. I've seen many self-serving, non-transparent decisions enacted by our supposed leaders, causing me to lose faith in our BOS."*

Former supervisor candidate Donald Simpson was always very civic-minded. Having lived in Pocono Township for most of his life, this active volunteer fireman served as Treasurer of the Pocono Township Park Board and as President, Financial Secretary and Fire Chief of the Pocono Township Fire Company. His history of contributions to his community had proven more than generous.

[9] Guidry, M., "Pocono's supervisors misgovern township" In Your Opinion, Pocono Record (10/18/2013) http://www.poconorecord.com/apps/pbcs.dll/article?AID=/20131018/NEWS04/310180318/-1/NEWS0401

Donald believed that five individuals were needed to oversee the community. *"It became clear that those individuals should not be employees"* and that a township manager was needed *"to run operations according to rules and regulations, for all."*

Verizon Construction Manager Richard Wielebinski, a 23-year township resident, felt that leadership needed to focus more on the future growth of Pocono Township.

Former New Yorker and 3-year Pocono Township resident Debra Morrishow came to our township meetings with enough prior civic experience to immediately see that things weren't right. She had been a member of *Community Board 10* in New York, whose purpose was to make sure all city services were available to residents and businesses of Central Harlem.

"After attending my first township meeting I was very surprised to learn that three people were in charge of making decisions for such a large township. I attended meeting after meeting and listened to the public express their concerns about different issues and it seemed the men in charge wouldn't or were unable to make acceptable decisive decisions. I knew something had to be done but I thought my only recourse was to vote them out of office at the next election. But when two of the supervisors voted one supervisor out of his paid position as the township road master and voted one of themselves in as road master I was mad. Then, to find out he was not qualified for the position as road master and that he was requesting about $20,000 more in pay, I knew I couldn't wait for the election to roll around."

Linda Kresge had been active in local issues for many of the 50 years she lived in Tannersville, Pennsylvania. Like many residents, she was dismayed with how Werkheiser was treated and believed it to be detrimental to good governing for supervisors to be able to appoint themselves to jobs paid for by taxpayers. Part of her published letter in the Pocono Record said it well.

Sign petition to make Pocono Township first class
In Your Opinion—Pocono Record

Second Class Townships were meant for small rural communities. As populations grow, the challenges within townships become more complicated and the old ways of doing business no longer make sense. When elected leaders can vote themselves into paid township jobs, there are no checks and balances. There's no transparency. They become their own boss and, as we have seen, that can cause intentional and/or unintentional abuses of power. We have also seen that the three-supervisor governing structure can create two-to-one conflicts that are obviously detrimental to streamlined and effective governing.[10]—**Linda Kresge**

Linda and Roy Smith, operators of Central Pocono Ambulance Association joined the group following an unsuccessful attempt by Supervisor Hess to defund their non-profit organization which had operated in Pocono Township and surrounding areas for over 50 years.[11]

According to Roy, *"Linda and I became aware of the group effort because of the troubles Frank Hess started with Central Pocono Ambulance. We believed Frank was using our organization in an attempt to get back at [former supervisor] Jane Cilurso. She had always been very supportive of our organization, and it's very obvious Frank held a great deal of ill will toward her, and seemed hell-bent on harming her or her supporters in any way he could. By listening to members of the group at a number of township meetings, we found people who felt the same as we do: that our present elected officials were not acting in the best interests of the township. As we learned more about the group, we quickly*

[10] Kresge, L., "Sign petition to make Pocono Township first class" In Your Opinion, Pocono Record (6/30/13): http://www.poconorecord.com/apps/pbcs.dll/article?AID=/20130630/NEWS04/306300312/-1/NEWSLETTER100

[11] Central Pocono Ambulance Association, Inc. Website: http://www.poconotownship.org/AMBULANCE.html

realized that we weren't alone in our feelings, and that we needed to add our support to the group's efforts. We were hesitant at first because of concerns that our efforts would be held against Central Pocono, but we decided that we had every right, as township residents, to show our support."

While they felt that Hess's attempt to defund the Central Pocono Ambulance was a personal vendetta, it wasn't the only driving force behind their involvement. The Werkheiser situation and other decisions made by the majority supervisors reinforced their belief that the BOS was on the wrong track.

"To me, they lost sight of the fact that they were elected to act in a manner that upheld the best interests of the township. Fairness and consistency was non-existent. Instead, they disregarded or misinterpreted many policies and procedures meant to ensure unbiased government."

John Bramley, a highly skilled cabinet maker and the owner of Bramley's Custom Cabinets, had been appointed township supervisor by Jane Cilurso and Harold Werkheiser in 2008 to fill a void created by the resignation of supervisor Willard "Nipper" Anglemyer. He would hold that position until 2010 when he would lose his re-election bid to Frank Hess, who was backed by CCPT.

Prior to his appointment as supervisor, Bramley served for seven years as Planning Commissioner and, after that, as a representative for the Pocono/Jackson Township Water Authority and 2nd Vice President of Central Pocono Ambulance. John was certainly no stranger to public service.

Like Roy and Linda Smith, he had reason to be upset by the attempt to defund the ambulance company and he was equally bothered by the constant infighting between the three current supervisors. He recalled when serving with Cilurso and Werkheiser, *"We had disagreements on some issues but we never argued. We always worked things out together."*

His disillusionment with the current BOS and their recent decisions placed him on track with many other residents and he was happy to join the group.

Born in the Cayman Islands, Maxine Turbolski has lived in the Pocono Mountains for 42 years, most of that time in Pocono Township. She and her husband owned and operated a campground in Tobyhanna, Pennsylvania and later, a laundromat in Mt. Pocono. After selling both businesses, she was employed for 15 years as secretary for the Pocono Mountain School District and has since retired. She and good friend Ruth Perfetti had been attending school board meetings together for a couple of years and they both began going to township meetings in early 2011.

Looking ten years younger than her 80 years, Ruth Perfetti was born and raised in the Pocono Mountains and is a graduate of East Stroudsburg High School. She retired in 1998 after a 40 year career with Acme Markets, a chain of 112 supermarkets founded in 1891 and now operating in Pennsylvania, New Jersey, Delaware and Maryland.[12] In 2013, Ruth was performing secretarial work for Hillcrest Farms, once a family resort and now a nursing home.

Maxine and Ruth were both unhappy with the BOS under the leadership of Jane Cilurso and when Henry Bengel was running to fill her seat they, like many other voters, thought him to be an alternative to what Maxine saw as the *"old boy network."* Bengel, with strong financial backing from CCPT, campaigned for transparency and better government and both Maxine and Ruth enthusiastically supported his run for office, at one point even attending a CCPT meeting. Bengel's opponent, Donald Simpson, was certainly not part of the *"old boy network,"* but he was a near-lifetime resident of the township and the two friends thought it wiser to vote for an outsider. In time, they could not have been more disappointed with their decision. Transparency and better government was far from what they would see.

Soon after, they joined forces with those seeking a better option.

Born and raised in Stroudsburg, Pennsylvania, retired truck driver Jake Singer lived in Pocono Township for close to 40 years and has served on the board of Central Pocono Ambulance.

---

12 Acme Market Website: http://acmemarkets.com/our-company/
traditions-history/

It had only been within the past couple of years that he found himself attending supervisor meetings. He had previously voted for Hess and then for Bengel but, like many other residents, felt betrayed by their leadership decisions. When campaigning, Bengel had promised not to appoint himself to a township job and eventually did just that. Hess supported the self-appointment, forcing Werkheiser out of his road master position and that rubbed Jake the wrong way. Not only was he morally outraged, believing you should never treat people with such disrespect and disdain, he was also a lifetime acquaintance of Werkheiser and didn't like seeing his friend treated in that manner.

When he heard about the group, it took no arm twisting to get him onboard.

Three generations of Roger Hanna's family were raised in the Pocono Mountains and Roger himself had been a township resident for 43 years.

"Pocono Township is the geographic center of Monroe County and the Pocono area. Route 611 is one of the main corridors through the Poconos and runs through the middle of our township. Our residents and businessmen deserve bright government leaders to help make the decisions relating to the unprecedented growth of our township."

He also believed that, while the supervisors were working very hard, for the most part *"their time and efforts left little time to plan and implement improvements for the future."*

Roger saw the need for more transparent and altruistic leadership. He felt strongly that change was essential.

It was a diverse group of average, community-minded individuals with no personal agendas. Team members included those of varying ages, gender, religion, ethnicity, occupation and political affiliation. (As for political affiliation, not once was personal politics ever discussed within the group. It's important to note that it was a non-issue.)

Everyone was aware of the problems within our BOS but no one was motivated by a desire to cast blame. Everyone simply wanted to research options and find a better way forward. The common belief was that change was in order.

Several members of our group researched what options were available to Pocono Township and it was found that we had three: we could go to a five member BOS, home rule or first class. The group discussed the pros and cons of each and the decision was made to try elevating our township to first class status.

A name was needed for the group and "Pocono First Initiative" (PFI) was decided upon.

Our motto: "*A first class township for a bright future.*"

CHAPTER 7
FIRST CLASS & TOWNSHIP
COMMISSIONERS

According to the Pennsylvania First Class Township Code,[13] in order for an existing township to become first class, its population must be at least 300 inhabitants per square mile. (When the time came, we would request and receive the required population certification from the county commissioner's office.) A referendum must be placed on the ballot during the municipal election and, in order to get that referendum on the ballot, a petition would have to be signed by at least 5% of registered voters. (PFI's petition would need 355 signatures.)

The voters would determine the outcome on Election Day. If a majority favored the referendum, officers of the current second class government would be terminated and a county court would select an interim board of commissioners to serve until the next municipal election, along with any other elected officers to which the township is entitled.

The number of commissioners is determined by population. (Pocono Township would have a board of five.) Those selected would begin their terms on the first Monday of January following the election. After the interim period and at the next municipal election, voters would elect five new commissioners as well as the other officers. Three of these newly elected commissioners would serve four-year terms and the other two, two-year terms. This overlapping of terms allows for steady transitions at election time by assuring there will always be experienced commissioners remaining on the board when new ones are elected. After this initial election, commissioners would all serve four-year terms. (PFI believes that four-year terms create greater accountability and expand the pool of talent to

---

[13]   PA. State Legislature Website, First Class Township Code: http://www. legis.state.pa.us/WU01/LI/LI/US/HTM/1931/0/0331. HTM

individuals willing to serve their township, but who do not desire a six-year term.)

Commissioner pay is set by law, depending on township population. (Pocono Township falls into the population category of 10,000-14,999 residents, which equates to a maximum compensation of $3,250 per year.)

Unlike supervisors in a second class township, commissioners are not allowed to hold paid township jobs. (PFI feels strongly that this restriction frees up financial resources to hire needed professionals, rather than depending on elected officials appointing themselves or others who may not have the qualifications necessary for a given position.[14])

According to the Pennsylvania Township Commissioner's Handbook,[15] to serve as a commissioner, one must be a registered voter and a township resident. They must reside within the township continuously for at least one year before their election and must retain their residence within the township. Before entering office, they must take an oath or affirmation of office, administered by a judge, district magistrate or notary public. He or she must swear to support the Constitution of the United States and of the Commonwealth of Pennsylvania and to faithfully perform the duties of the office. The State Ethics Act requires them to file financial interest statements each year while in office and one year after leaving.

Commissioners play a central role in township government. The general supervision of the township is in their hands. They serve as the legislative body of the township—setting policy, enacting ordinances and resolutions, adopting budgets and levying taxes. In townships not employing a professional manager, commissioners may also perform executive functions such as formulating the budget, enforcing ordinances, approving expenditures and hiring employees. In some townships, they play a large role in administrative activities and oversee the day-to-day operation of township government.

---

[14]   Pocono First Initiative Website: http://poconofirst.org/facts/
[15]   PA. Township Commissioner's Handbook: http://www.newpa.com/webfm_send/1519

They are also viewed as community leaders. They are the proper recipients of complaints, ideas and suggestions concerning township affairs. In many cases, the commissioner is called upon to serve as a problem solver, acting as an agent for township citizens with the municipality and/or outside agencies. The commissioner has a role in representing the township's communal interests—past, present and future. Although assisted by a Planning Commission or paid administrator, final decisions are made by commissioners.

Functioning in the best interest of the township is a must. Commissioners have the authority to enact legislation covering governmental functions such as health, fire and police protection as well as taxation. They have a statutory duty to repair and maintain public roads and the power to regulate and control collection, removal and disposal of solid waste. They are involved in the fiscal management of the township and are not only responsible for raising the necessary money through taxes, service charges and grants, but also for seeing that municipal funds are spent in accordance with the established budget and capital program. They also have the authorization to make and adopt all ordinances, bylaws, rules and regulations deemed necessary for the proper management and control of the township, in order to maintain good government and protect the safety and welfare of its citizens.

Commissioners represent the township and are expected to be concerned with and, at times, to attempt to influence state legislation affecting their municipality. As representatives of the township, they are in a position to exert some influence on the decisions of state legislators.

In addition to the power to deliberate, formulate and enact local legislation and regulations, commissioners have quasi-judicial powers as a hearing board to hear arguments, interpret local ordinances and decide certain issues. The formulation of legislative policy involves full and free public discussion of issues, often with a commissioner vigorously acting as advocate for a particular policy approach or possibly spearheading opposition. Such activity is often a necessary part of the legislative process.

The First Class Township Code requires commissioners to meet at least once a month at a time and place designated by the board.

What is the role of a Township Commissioner?

QUALIFICATIONS:
- Be a registered voter and township resident.
- Reside within the township continuously for at least one year before his/her election and must retain residence within the township.
- Take an oath or affirmation of office, administered by a judge, district magistrate, or notary public before entering office.
- File annual financial interest statements per the State Ethics Act, a standard procedure for all township officials.

RESPONSIBILITIES:
- Set policy, enact ordinances and resolutions, adopt budgets and levy taxes.
- Fiscal management of the township – raising money through taxes, service charges and grants.
- Disburse funds in accordance with the approved budget and capital program.
- Enact legislation covering governmental functions such as health, fire and police protection.
- Ensures the repair and maintenance of public roads and disposal of solid waste.
- Appoint volunteer boards to advise and recommend in various areas of government decision-making.
- Hire competent and trained employees to operate the day-to-day business of the township.

COMMUNITY LEADERSHIP:
- Problem solving and conflict mediation.
- Represent the township's community interests.
- Serve on special subcommittees or regional municipal groups.
- Express township needs to state officials when necessary.

*First Class Township Code requires commissioners to meet at least once a month at a time and place designated by the board.

Handout distributed by PFI.

The Pocono First Initiative studied the First Class Township Code and the Pennsylvania Township Commissioner's Handbook. Everything we learned led us to the conclusion that Pocono Township could surely benefit from such a governing structure.

The hard work was about to begin.

A governing body for PFI was needed and it was time for us to vote for officers. Judi, a natural leader and the driving force behind the group, was the obvious choice for chairwoman and our vote for her was unanimous. No one doubted that Monica Gerrity, also a driving force, should be assistant chairwoman and that too was a unanimous decision. Donald Simpson was voted in as treasurer, Taylor Munoz as communication director and Marie Guidry as secretary. Diane Zweifel was placed in charge of our "press machine," her responsibility being to keep letters to the editor flowing to the newspaper. She would be instrumental in encouraging letter writing in support of first class. I wasn't voted in to any position but decided that my contribution would be to write some of those letters.

We formed a Political Action Committee (PAC).

According to Taylor, "*The PAC was necessary for solidifying our group's purpose and providing a centralized entity for receiving and recording financial investments and paying for campaign materials. In other words, PACs provide a means for raising and spending money to support or defeat a candidate or cause. It also provides an element of transparency for the group and greater public, since all receipts and disbursements must be recorded and reported to the Monroe County Elections Office. It helps prevent and discourage any impression of fiscal impropriety and keep account of the group's activities.*"

How we were going to finance our efforts was an important decision that needed to be made. It was the belief of most members of PFI that we should not take money from outside interests but, instead, finance everything through our own small personal donations. At the same time, we would have to be frugal with our expenses and try to get the most bang for each of our bucks. That's just what we did. By the time our journey was to end in November, only $2,500 would be spent by PFI and all of it would be from our own small personal donations as well as several equally small donations from a few of our friends and relatives.

We made a decision for our team to meet each week and forged a plan of action.

A website was built (poconofirst.org). Business cards and a large PFI banner displaying the website address were ordered. The banner would be displayed in high trafficked areas within the township by supportive businesses, affording it constant and prolonged visibility.

Plans were made to have postcards and other promotional materials printed when needed. A few months later, fifty yard signs would also be ordered and strategically placed throughout the township by team members.

From the start, the decision was made to take the high road through the entire process. We expected opposition from CCPT, knowing they would fight hard to maintain the status-quo. Regardless, we vowed to proudly "play nice" from start to finish, focusing only on what was in the best interest of Pocono Township.

A press conference was held in front of the Pocono Township Municipal Building in Tannersville to introduce PFI to the public and announce our intentions. Attended by about two-dozen supportive residents and local press, this gathering was the beginning of a six-month public relations and educational campaign to elevate Pocono Township to first class.

Press conference at Pocono Township Municipal Building.

Already we had established PFI as a PAC, elected officers for our team, designed and ordered promotional material, built a website, secured an email address and phone number, set up weekly PFI meetings, built an effective press machine and mapped a forward-looking plan of action.

That plan of action was developed based in part on the process used by Lower Macungie Township in Pennsylvania when they moved to first class in 2007. They made the change after "more than $2.5 million was allegedly embezzled from township sewer funds and a former supervisor, Marge Szulborski, was charged with stealing it between 1999 and 2006 while serving as the full-time sewer department director in addition to being an elected supervisor."[16] The residents formed their own grassroots organization, *Citizens for Change*, and ultimately became a first class township. PFI reached out to former and current officials of Lower Macungie Township and, thankfully, they were very willing to share their expertise. That helped point us in the right direction.

To get the first class referendum on the November 2013 ballot it was legally required to obtain 355 petition signatures, as that number represented 5% of our registered voters. However, we wanted the petition to represent an overwhelming desire for change by our fellow residents and we set our goal at 600 signatures.

The petition had to be submitted to the county court by August 3rd at the latest. Our plan was to begin the petition drive on May 21st, Primary Election Day, and that would give us about ten weeks to achieve our ambitious goal.

Schedules were set up for PFI members to man the polls with petitions on the 21st of May. There were three locations that needed covering and most of our twenty team members volunteered for duty. By the end of Primary Day the general feeling was one of optimism.

Most voters with whom our team spoke were receptive to the idea of change. Residents who vote in municipal elections, especially primary elections, are generally those who regularly pay attention to what is going on in their community. They read the local newspaper and they watch their local television news. It did appear that many voters knew what had been transpiring in Pocono Township over the past couple of years.

---

[16] Lower Macungie Township Citizens for Change Website: http://www.lmtcitizensforchange.org/truly_first_class.cfm

Naturally, there were some skeptics as well and we certainly expected that. There was also a troubling indication that CCPT had initiated a campaign of opposition to first class in an effort to keep the status-quo. Several of our members were told by voters at the polls that they had been told not to sign the petition. Others said they heard that, should first class pass, taxes would increase. That was intentionally deceptive and an obvious scare tactic. This campaign of misinformation and half-truths would not only continue, it would aggressively grow as we inched toward the November municipal election.

Thanking the many residents signing the petition on Primary Day, Diane wrote her own letter to the editor which was published in the Pocono Record.

Sign to make Pocono a first class township
In Your Opinion—Pocono Record

Thank you, residents of Pocono Township. Pocono First Initiative members are encouraged by the number of registered voters in Pocono Township who came out on Primary Day to vote in the primary elections and to sign the petition to have the question, "Shall the township of Pocono become a township of the First Class?" placed on the November 2013 ballot.

By putting your signature on this petition, you are allowing the people of Pocono Township to decide in November whether they want to change their form of government from a second-class township to a first-class township. With a first-class township, there would be five commissioners, with each commissioner's salary capped at $3,250 per year as specified in the first-class code provision and who would serve four-year terms. This conceivably could be a better form of government for our community moving forward. I hope enough signatures will be obtained and the question will appear on the November ballot, which will let the people of the township decide.[17]—**Diane Zweifel**

Following Primary Day, we had team members with petitions regularly stationed at several of our local post offices. We determined that Saturday mornings would see the most traffic, as people had only until noon to take care of their postal needs. On Saturdays from 9am until 12pm, PFI was a presence at the Tannersville, Scotrun and Swiftwater Post Offices. Along with obtaining signatures, our mission was to educate our fellow residents as to the benefits of first class.

It wasn't long before we attained the legally required 355 signatures. For the next few weeks we stayed the course, looking to reach our 600 signature goal.

In the meantime, the following letter appeared in the Pocono Record.

Support Pocono's First Class Initiative
In Your Opinion—Pocono Record

Many have signed the First Class Initiative petition and it's likely the question "Should Pocono Township become a first-class township?" will be on the November ballot.

First-class townships are governed by five elected commissioners. They're not allowed to work for the township, therefore leaving additional finances to hire necessary professional services to address the complex needs of a growing township.

Five different perspectives and the no-job rule will result in more informed, transparent and independent decision-making for residents. A five-member board and no-job rule will eliminate the two-against-one conflicts we've seen.

---

[17]   Zweifel, D., "Sign to make Pocono a first class township" In Your Opinion, Pocono Record (5/29/13) http://www.poconorecord.com/apps/pbcs.dll/article?AID=/20130529/NEWS04/305290305

Many watched with frustration as Frank Hess was kept out of the loop for his first years as supervisor. Many more were angered when Henry Bengel and Hess voted Harold Werkheiser out of his job, only to vote Bengel in. The resulting lawsuit will cost the township thousands in legal fees.

Situations like those must be eliminated. With the no-job rule, you'll attract public servants whose focus is solely on the township. With a five-commissioner board, you'll minimize the effects of campaign donations, so it wouldn't be likely that a majority of commissioners could be beholden to the same influential backers. (Local politics is no different than national.)

Opposition to the initiative is small, but vocal. It's being said by some who disagree, that taxes will increase as a result of this change. There is no basis, nor historical data, for this claim. Taxes are driven by services provided by the township. As long as we elect financially responsible people, we can continue to hold costs down and lower taxes.

The First Class Initiative is the way to go. Five different perspectives and the no-job rule indeed will result in more informed, transparent and independent decision-making on behalf of Pocono Township residents. The time is right for First Class.[18]—**Jack Swersie**

In the end, 630 Pocono Township residents wanted to see the question "Shall the Township of Pocono become a Township of the First Class?" on the November ballot. By early July, a few weeks before the deadline, our petition was submitted to the county court.

We were all pleased and this letter to the editor expressed our hopes:

---

[18]   Swersie, J., "Support Pocono's first class initiative" In Your Opinion, Pocono Record (6/4/13) http://www.poconorecord.com/apps/pbcs.dll/article?AID=/20130604/NEWS04/306040312/-1/news16

Support going first class in Pocono Twp.
In Your Opinion—Pocono Record

Pocono First Initiative filed its petition with the court and waits to see whether the referendum will appear on November's ballot. I'm concerned about the future of Pocono Township, and that's why I support the move to a first-class township.

Let's forget politics and personality and focus on making prudent decisions to properly manage our resources. Currently, supervisors hire people to fill full-time positions that have no job description. And, supervisors can't (or won't) fill the long-vacant road master job, one position that actually has a job description. Is there a plan to staff and manage the new sewer system? Do we know how much it will cost to implement the mandated recycling plan? Is there a long-term plan for maintaining roads and replacing police and road crew vehicles? All too often, supervisors respond to these public concerns with "I will take that under advisement." My fear is that the answer to all three is a resounding "no."

Have our supervisors done anything worth praising? Yes, they have. Full-time staffers have been replaced with part-timers to reflect the reduction in need for those services. And, supervisors have managed not to raise our taxes for the last two years. But, 2014 leadership must do better. We face complex challenges and rising costs. We need leaders who work well together. They need to plan for our future without being sidetracked by politics. Most importantly, they must conduct business in a fair and open manner. Moving to a first-class structure is the way to accomplish this.

Let's start 2014 with a board of five commissioners who are committed to setting the right policies and hiring qualified people to run daily township business. We can and must do better if we are going to avoid tax increases while providing all the requisite services.[19]—**Judi Coover**

COMMONWEALTH OF PENNSYLVANIA

PETITION

To have Question for Pocono Township Printed upon the Official Ballot
For the Municipal Election, November 5, 2013

We the undersigned, all of whom are qualified electors of Monroe County and Pocono Township, hereby petition the Court of Common Pleas of Monroe County to have the following Question.

Shall the Township of Pocono become a Township of the First Class?

printed upon the Official Ballot in the Township of Pocono for the municipal election for the year 2013.

	SIGNATURE OF ELECTOR	PRINTED NAME OF ELECTOR	HOUSE#	PLACE OF RESIDENCE STREET OR ROAD	TOWNSHIP	DATE OF SIGNING
1						
2						
3						
4						
5						
6						
7						
8						
9						
10						
11						
12						
13						
14						
15						
16						
17						
18						
19						
20						

Commonwealth of Pennsylvania Petition.

---

[19]   Coover, J., "Support going first class in Pocono Twp." In Your Opinion, Pocono Record (7/29/13) http://www.poconorecord.com/apps/pbcs.dll/article?AID=/20130729/NEWS04/307290315/-1/NEWSLETTER100

CHAPTER 10
SCARE TACTICS AND TAXES

The fear mongering by the opposition started increasing once it appeared likely that PFI was going to get the first class referendum on the November ballot. When it comes to scaring the public, nothing works better than screaming *"Your taxes are going to increase!"* That scream would become a roar as CCPT ramped up their efforts to discourage residents from supporting first class. Now through Election Day, the tax scare wouldn't be the only cry coming from the opposition, but at this time it was the most prominent and certainly the loudest.

It was also far from the truth!

As far back as June 3rd at the BOS Monday night meeting, Frank Hess even used this strategy in an unsuccessful attempt to scare residents away from supporting the measure. When asked by a resident what his opinion was on first class, he contended that it could make it possible to double the local tax rate.[20]

His contention reflected either a lack of knowledge about tax-related matters concerning first and second class townships in Pennsylvania or a fear of first class becoming a reality in Pocono Township. People thought it was both.

If one reads the Pennsylvania first and second class township codes, it is clear that the cap on allowable taxes in a second class township is actually higher than the cap in a first class township. A picture of the truth was painted by Jake Singer in yet another letter to the editor.

---

[20] Pierce, D., "Taxing issues if change in class happens" Pocono Record (6/9/13) http://www.poconorecord.com/apps/pbcs.dll/article?AID=/20130609/NEWS/306090330

Know what drives local tax rates
In Your Opinion—Pocono Record

The June 9th article titled "Taxing issues if change in class happens" by David Pierce can easily confuse readers as to whether changing from a Second Class to a First Class Township would raise taxes in Pocono Township.

To clarify the issue one should look only at the combined (general, emergency and parks/recreation) millage rate allowed by Pennsylvania code. Pierce said "All told, a first-class township could raise combined property taxes to 34.1 mills and a second-class township could raise combined taxes to 38. 5."

For Frank Hess to say that a First Class Township could conceivable double the local tax rate is disingenuous. Pocono Township currently has a combined tax millage rate of 17.35 when, by Second Class code, it could be as high as 38.5. That's proof that a cap on allowable tax rates does not in any way mean that taxes will increase to that level. Mr. Hess should know that, as he, his fellow supervisors, and all the supervisors prior to them have kept the local tax rate well below the 38.5 cap.

In short, it's NOT the cap on allowable tax rates that determine our local taxes. Rates are determined by services provided by the township. As long as we elect fiscally responsible people to leadership positions, there is no reason to believe that taxes will increase in a First Class Township.

There are those who stand to lose power and influence should we go to First Class. Their only line of defense has been to spread the word of possible higher taxes. But facts should put this matter to rest.[21]—**Jake Singer**

Sadly, when it came to the opposition, facts meant very little and the drumbeat of higher taxes would continue clear through Election Day.

First Class vs. Second Class Comparison	First Class	Second Class
Supervisors or Commissioners	Commissioners	Supervisors
Number on Board	5	3
Can hold Township jobs?	No	Yes
Millage Rates		
General Purpose	30.00	14.00
Fire House	3.00	
Lighting		5.00
Trees	0.10	
50% of #1 Assessment		7.00
Township Buildings	Unlimited	
Fire House & Equipment		3.00
Debt	Unlimited	Unlimited
Fire Hydrants		2.00
Retirement	0.50	
Recreation	Unlimited	Unlimited
Emergency Services	0.50	0.50
Revolving Fund		5.00
Road Equipment Fund		2.00
Total Millage (Not including unlimited)	34.10	38.50

---

[21] Singer, J. "Know what drives local tax rates" In Your Opinion, Pocono Record (6/23/13) http://www.poconorecord.com/apps/pbcs.dll/article?AID=/20130623/NEWS04/306230310/-1/NEWSLETTER100

CHAPTER 11

MEETING WITH THE OPPOSITION

Long before the courts validated our petition and officially confirmed that the first class referendum would appear on the November ballot, PFI had discussed the need to hold public forums to educate the residents of Pocono Township so they could make an informed Election Day decision regarding first class. We felt it unnecessary to hold these events until after we received official court confirmation, so we did not yet schedule any dates.

At the July 2nd township meeting Hess announced that the BOS would be holding their own educational forum in July to discuss the merits of first and second class townships. What Hess didn't know was that PFI was aware that members of CCPT were also planning a forum and had taken a trip to the state capital in Harrisburg that same day "to discuss the matter with state officials with broad knowledge of the state township codes."[22]

Naturally it was suspected by those at the meeting that Hess and CCPT were planning the forum together in an attempt to thwart the success of first class. When confronted, he denied knowing anything about the trip to Harrisburg, saying that the planned forum was his idea and his idea alone. But few in attendance at the meeting believed him.

He would eventually have his own forum, but not until a week before the November election. It would be then that anyone who may have had doubts that Hess and CCPT were indeed planning the event together would have those doubts put to rest.

---

[22]   Pierce, D. "World class fight over first-class over twp. status", Pocono Record (7/3/13) http://www.poconorecord.com/apps/pbcs.dll/article?AID=/20130703/NEWS/307030326/-1/rss21

On July 3rd, a couple of CCPT members, in an attempt to smooth out the controversy surrounding Hess's announcement of the BOS forum, contacted Judi and asked for a meeting. Judi invited them over to her home that evening where, during a very cordial and respectful conversation, they suggested to Judi that she combine PFI's plans with theirs and hold a joint forum to debate the pros and cons of first class versus second class townships. PFI had already discussed the idea of a debate format and that was a no-go from the start. A debate seemed senseless. We already knew the pros and cons of a second class township as did many residents of Pocono Township. We were living it! Our objective was to educate our fellow residents on the merits of first class, which we all believed to be a better governing option for the township. Judi expressed our views and the meeting ended with CCPT indicating that they would be going forward with their own forum.

But it's amazing how quickly things can change.

The next day, Pocono Record columnist Howard Frank, in a scathing column titled "Carnival coming to Pocono Township?" wrote, *"Don't be fooled by false prophets who come to you in sheep's clothing. They may be ravening wolves."*

He went on to reveal that the forum planned by CCPT would showcase officials from the Pennsylvania State Association of Township Supervisors which is a state-wide lobbying agency that represents only second-class townships.

Frank stated, *"If* [they] *bring in anyone from the association,* [they are] *bringing in a shill."* Frank concluded his column with, *"But for Pocono Township residents, it's buyer beware. They are the buyer and* [CCPT] *is the seller."* [23]

It appeared that their efforts were backfiring. Bad publicity for them and their businesses was the last thing they wanted. Hours after the newspaper hit the stands, Judi received a phone call from CCPT letting her know that they were not going forward with their event.

---

[23]   Frank, H., Frankly Speaking column "Carnival coming to Pocono Township", Pocono Record (7/4/13) http://www.poconorecord.com/apps/pbcs.dll/article?AID=/20130704/NEWS/307040338/-1/NEWS040301

But Howard Frank was right. Although we were more than aware of it ourselves, in time others would see it first-hand; those in sheep's clothing might well be *"ravening wolves!"*[24]

---

[24] Frank, H., Frankly Speaking column "Carnival coming to Pocono Township", Pocono Record (7/4/13) http://www.poconorecord.com/apps/pbcs.dll/article?AID=/20130704/NEWS/307040338/-1/NEWS040301

CHAPTER 12
PETITION VALIDATION

It would be another couple of weeks before PFI would receive the court order validating our petition and our focus remained on the future. We continued to have people posted at the local post offices on Saturday mornings, distributing literature and explaining first class to those who were willing to listen.

And of those coming and going, there were many who knew the importance of what we were trying to achieve and showed unqualified support for our work. There were also those who were resentful of our efforts and happy to express their contempt. Luckily, that was minimal but many of those who did resent us cited the possibility of higher taxes as their main concern. A few actually asserted that our group was opposed to the current BOS because the majority supervisors were New Yorkers. Considering that a number of us were also from New York, their assertions were not only untrue but laughable as well.

At the July 11th PFI meeting, Judi announced that she had contacted Bethlehem Township officials. Bethlehem Township, located in the city of Bethlehem in Northampton County, Pennsylvania about 30 miles south of Pocono Township, boasts a population over two times the size of ours and has been a first class township since January 1st, 1963.[25] After speaking with Bethlehem's then township manager, Howard Kutzler, Judi made arrangements for a small group of PFI team members to attend one of their Monday night Board of Commissioners meetings and on July 15th five of us made the trip to Bethlehem. We could not have been more pleased that we did.

---

[25] Bethlehem Township, Pennsylvania Website: http://www. bethlehemtwp.com/btweb/

Every one of us was impressed with Howard, who not only had an abundance of knowledge about township issues but an enthusiasm and love for the work he was performing. The general consensus after attending the meeting and then speaking at length with Howard and briefly with one of their commissioners, was that there was a level of professionalism exhibited by their leaders that we needed in Pocono Township.

Once the court order was issued for the referendum to be placed on the November ballot, we publicly announced we would be holding three educational forums: one in August, another in September and the last in October, just a couple of weeks shy of the election. The objective would be to let residents know why we felt that first class would be the best move forward for Pocono Township. Our first event would be held at St. Paul Lutheran Church in Tannersville on August 28th. Dates and locations of the other two were tentatively set and our focus was now on developing the format of our first.

It was decided the length of the presentation should not exceed 90-minutes. Judi would provide opening remarks, Monica would moderate, Taylor would inform residents of what first class is and why we felt it to be right for the township's future and four of our members would make short statements expressing their personal convictions for first class. Bethlehem Township Manager Howard Kutzler was to be our featured speaker and he would make his presentation next. That would be followed by a question/answer session paneled by Taylor, Scott, Judi and Howard.

We had about a month to promote this forum and we used that time wisely, posting the upcoming event on our website, sending out press releases and writing letters to the Pocono Record. Our press machine, under the capable leadership of Diane, was very efficient and word spread fast.

With the question now officially on the ballot, our first forum planned and promoted and the general mood of township residents being positive toward first class, it was looking more likely that PFI might very well be successful in getting the referendum passed.

Concern was growing within CCPT and they once again approached Judi, asking for a meeting. A get-together at the home of a CCPT member was scheduled. Now it would be incumbent upon Judi to convince PFI members to attend and that was not going to be an easy task. The level of trust toward CCPT was low and there was strong resentment between some PFI members and the opposition. Judi was able to convince only seven of our twenty members to attend.

On July 24th the two sides met. Like the first meeting with the opposition on July 3rd, interaction between the parties was marked by cordiality. According to Judi, PFI allowed them to guide the evening agenda and they started by asking questions of our group. It appeared they wanted to get a better understanding of PFI's motivation, and it became clear to them after their questions were answered that it wasn't personal animosity toward the township leadership that drove PFI, but rather a sincere and studied belief that first class was the right move forward for Pocono Township.

By the meeting's end, CCPT promised they would not organize against the first class referendum. They would not oppose us. In the words of one of their members, "*It's time to press the reset button.*"

Promises can easily be broken.

CHAPTER 13
THE MAJORITY SUPERVISORS
GET NERVOUS

At the August 26th BOS meeting, two days prior to our first forum, Hess suggested that, as an alternative to first class, the township should consider a proposal increasing their three supervisor board to five. Pocono Record's David Pierce reported that Hess said there are too many unknown impacts in becoming a first-class township to make that switch in a little more than two months. *"This first-class township thing is too much of a leap right now,"* Hess said. *"I still don't think there's enough time for voters to learn all the implications."*[26]

That wasn't the first time he had suggested making changes to the second class township structure, nor would it be the last. Two weeks before, he presented the idea of passing a resolution that would forbid township supervisors from holding paid township jobs. Later, as the likelihood of first class becoming a reality would increase and as Election Day would draw closer, we would hear these suggestions repeated yet again.

It was clear to those in attendance when Hess made these proposals that it was a smoke-screen attempt on his part. He was trying to scare residents by labeling a change to first class as *"too much of a leap"* and he was trying to appease them by making it seem as though he could provide the same results by simply passing resolutions. Knowing that if first class passed he would no longer be supervisor, it appeared he was simply trying to hold on to his job. Pocono Township residents saw through the smoke. In a sharply worded letter in the Pocono Record titled "No wonder supervisor opposes initiative," a township resident said it best.

---

[26]   Pierce, D. "Wednesday: First forum on first class proposal" Pocono Record (8/27/13) http://www.poconorecord.com/apps/pbcs.dll/article?AID=/20130827/NEWS/308270341/-1/NEWSLETTER100

No wonder supervisor opposes initiative
In Your Opinion—Pocono Record

In David Pierce's Aug. 27 article, "Wednesday: First forum on first-class proposal," Supervisor Chairman Frank Hess suggests going from a three-member to a five-member supervisor's board as an alternative to the First Class Initiative, which will be on November's ballot. He cites the uncertainty of going to first class: "This first-class township thing is too much of a leap," Hess said. "I still don't think there's enough time" for voters to learn all the implications.

Not enough time? The First Class Initiative idea has been floated for four months now. Voters have done their research and more than 600 of them signed the petition to get the referendum on the ballot. This isn't brain surgery. One only has to do an online search to access and read the Pennsylvania First Class Township Code or go to poconofirst.org to read the Pennsylvania Township Commissioners Handbook. The Pocono First group is also sponsoring educational forums during the next two months. There has been, and continues to be, plenty of time for voters to learn the implications if they haven't done so already.

And to what "implications" is Mr. Hess even referring? He's already publicly stated at a township meeting that he wanted to propose a resolution to restrict township supervisors from holding paid township jobs. Now, he says he'd like to expand the board to five supervisors. Those two ideas are the hallmark of a first-class township. (Five commissioners who would not be paid township employees.) If Hess truly supported those ideas, one would logically conclude that he would also support the First Class Initiative.

But Mr. Hess does not support the initiative. Nor has he acted upon his own suggestions. To do so would not be in his interest.[27]—**Jake Singer**

The question as to why the township should elevate to first class, rather than simply increasing the number of supervisors and prohibiting them from taking township jobs, was a legitimate question which needed to be asked. And it would be asked—and clearly answered—two days later at our first educational forum.

[27]   Singer, J. "No wonder supervisor opposes initiative", In Your Opinion, Pocono Record (9/5/13)
http://www.poconorecord.com/apps/pbcs.dll/article?AID=/20130905/NEWS04/309050317/-1/NEWSLETTER100

POCONO FIRST INITIATIVE

Let the people decide...

What does becoming a first class township mean?
- Five elected Township Commissioners
- Four-year terms
- Commissioners cannot be employees of the township
- Elected officials and employees have distinct, separate roles and responsibilities

Vote _YES_ on November 5th for a better form of government that will help Pocono Township prepare to meet the complex challenges of our growing community

VOTE YES

We need leadership who will work to restore trust and encourage citizens to take part on their local government.

Pocono First Initiative will conduct three educational sessions:
→ August 28th at St Paul's Lutheran Church
→ Sept 24th at Our Lady Of Victory Church
→ Oct 24th at NCC Monroe Campus

All sessions begin at 7 pm

www.poconofirst.org
poconofirst@gmail.com

Literature distributed to residents at post office by PFI.

CHAPTER 14

THE FIRST EDUCATIONAL FORUM

When August 28th arrived, PFI was ready and, as evidenced by the 150 people in attendance at our first forum, so were the residents of Pocono Township. Included among those 150 attendees were our three supervisors, two of whom sat stoically throughout the session. Curiously absent from the gathering were any representatives from CCPT and that posed the question as to whether or not they really cared to learn the facts about first class. That question would be categorically answered two months later when, after all three of our forums were history, there still had been no CCPT presence.

Judi opened the evening, welcoming residents and informing them about the issues that brought PFI up to that moment. Monica took over as moderator and introduced Taylor who spent fifteen minutes discussing the intricacies of a first class township structure. Following Taylor's informative presentation, Scott, Roger, Richard and I, in short prepared statements, each shared our own personal reasons for wanting to see first class become a reality in Pocono Township. Monica then introduced Howard Kutzler, who made an inspired presentation and then joined Judi, Taylor and Scott on the panel to answer questions from our fellow residents.

The question/answer segment of the forum was impressive. Questions were answered by all with confidence and precision and it was obvious that the four individuals on the panel were well informed and well prepared.

One interesting question asked by a resident was, "What are the cons of going to first class?" Naturally, you can't expect supporters of this initiative to see any cons and that was honestly explained to the attendees. PFI believed that there was no downside to first class, unless change was a bad thing. We believed that change was not only good for Pocono Township, it was essential.

"*Why should we take the chance of changing to first class, when we could just increase the number of supervisors to five and prohibit them from taking paid township jobs?*" was another question posed by an attendee. That had to be answered in two parts. Judi tackled the first. "*Going from three to five supervisors only exasperates the problem of having elected officials who are also employees,*" she responded. "*Going to five could result in having five instead of three supervisors on the payroll, holding jobs they may or may not be qualified for and increasing the role ambiguity that results when you are your own boss. There would be five conflicted people instead of three.*"

As far as the second part of the question, prohibiting supervisors from holding paid township jobs, it was explained that the legality of that action was questionable since Pennsylvania code gives supervisors a legal right to appoint themselves to jobs. But legal or not, if a resolution is passed stating that supervisors cannot hold township jobs it would be just as easy for the current or future BOS to pass yet another resolution reversing the first and returning the township to business as usual.

The forum lasted just over the 90-minutes we had allotted ourselves and was an unqualified success. Pocono Record had been relentlessly reporting on PFI and the BOS, and their comprehensive coverage of our initiative continued with an article by David Pierce which appeared the following day.

Bethlehem Township official lays out first-class workings
By David Pierce—Pocono Record Writer

Elected officials in the first class township of Bethlehem set policy, but don't get involved in the daily implementation of that policy, Bethlehem Township Manager Howard Kutzler told a Pocono Township forum Wednesday.

Kutzler was the featured speaker at a forum sponsored by Pocono First Initiative, a political action committee that petitioned for a November Pocono Township voter referendum on whether Pocono should transition from a second class to a first class township.

Pocono currently is governed by three elected supervisors who serve six-year terms and can appoint themselves to township jobs. If the voter referendum is approved, Pocono will be governed by a five-member board of elected commissioners who serve four-year terms and will be prohibited from appointing themselves to township jobs.

But it would be up to Monroe County Court to appoint five residents who would oversee township operations during a two-year transitional period beginning in January.

First class townships have the option of appointing a manager to oversee township operations. Bethlehem Township commissioners don't manage employees and don't spend countless hours preparing annual budgets, Kutzler said. Those are among his duties, carried out with the board's approval.

"It is my job to report to the commissioners as a whole," and not to individual members, Kutzler told about 100 people, including three Pocono supervisors, gathered at St. Paul Lutheran Church. "They set the policy. It's my job to carry out those policies. "I basically try to do it in a straight line," he added."

Efficiency, competence and professionalism were what Pocono First Initiative members tried to convey as major reasons for becoming a first class township. A key component, members said, is the first class prohibition against elected officials naming themselves to township jobs.

"That is legal under the second class township code but I don't think it's a good idea," initiative member Jack Swersie said. "In fact I think it's a lousy idea."

When supervisors put themselves in township jobs, there are no checks and balances, he added. "They become their own boss." Swersie said.

Few supervisors have management backgrounds for the complex issues handled by a growing township like Pocono, added Scott Gilliland. "Sometimes we don't know what we don't know," Gilliland said. "Sometimes it's difficult to jump in and run the ship, so to speak."

"With the growth that continues here in the township it's really time for a change," added Rich Wielebinski. "Change is good. Change will move our township down the road."

A core group of about a dozen volunteers has been working on the first-class-township referendum since February. They collected nearly twice the required 355 voter signatures—five percent of registered voters—needed to get the first class question on the ballot.

The tightly scripted forum format included individual speakers, followed by a panel that answered written questions submitted on index cards. Asked why they didn't push for Pocono Township to become a five-member supervisors' board, rather than seeking a conversion to a first class township, Judi Coover said first class is the best of several options her group researched.

"The only option we have is what is set out in the first class code," she said.[28]—**David Pierce**

---

[28]   Pierce, D. "Bethlehem Township official lays out first-class workings" Pocono Record (8/29/13) http://www.poconorecord.com/apps/pbcs.dll/article?AID=/20130829/NEWS/308290333/-1/NEWSLETTER100

A couple of weeks before our September 24th educational forum, the Pocono Record contacted PFI asking if we would write an editorial in support of first class. Letters to the editor were allowed only 300 words but, due to the importance of the referendum as we neared the November election, the newspaper planned on devoting half a page to the topic. They requested 600-700 words and were going to provide a byline for the writer.

At the same time, they approached the opposition requesting an editorial focusing on why voters should reject the initiative.

There was no question that Judi should author the editorial for PFI and she set out to write what would turn out to be the most clearly-written, comprehensive and convincing argument in support of the change to first class.

On Sunday, September 22nd, the Pocono Record published her eloquently written opinion piece titled "Yes, Pocono residents deserve first class."

Yes, Pocono residents deserve first class
Editorial by Judi Coover—Pocono Record

As Pocono Township has grown and changed over time, so has its need for services, intelligent decision making, and balanced growth. In response, Pocono First Initiative® supports upgrading Pocono Township from a "second class township" to a "township of the first class." The following explanation clarifies what a first class township "is" and what it "is not."

In short, the first class township structure will modernize the way our township does business. First class townships are governed by a five-member board of commissioners who serve four-year terms and cannot be paid employees of the township. This stands in direct contrast with second class townships, where supervisors can appoint themselves to paid positions for which they lack the necessary experience, sign their own paychecks, and serve six-year terms (longer than any state and most federal elected officials).

With a five member board of commissioners, there is more sharing of responsibility and improved representation for the township and its citizens. Since commissioners cannot be employed by the township, tax dollars are instead used for qualified professional staff to handle day-to-day township tasks. The commissioners can then commit their attention to governing and setting policy.

Shorter terms, five diverse perspectives, and the stipulation that commissioners cannot be paid township employees result in more informed, transparent and independent decision-making.

Upgrading to a first class township will not raise taxes. Changing the form of government in no way leads to a tax increase, rather, the demand for services and township leadership does.

Pocono Township's budget already provides for a municipal police department—one of the biggest line items in any township's budget—a park, and operation of a sewer system. Changing to a first class township will not change the demand for services, but is likely to improve the efficiency of providing those services. In fact, more independent eyes on spending combined with qualified professionals who live locally handling the daily functioning of the Township is expected to result in increased savings.

Furthermore, according to first class township code, the maximum allowable millage rate for a first class township is 34.1 mills. In a second class township, the maximum millage rate is 38.5 mills. Both codes allow for unlimited mills in some spending areas, but the second class code has a higher combined mills rate.

Pocono Township's tax rate is 17.35 mills. Compare that to Harrison Township's (pop. 10,461) 5.3 mills, Hanover Township's (pop. 11,076) 5.5 mills, Hopewell Township's (pop. 12, 593) 14 mills, and so on. All are first class townships. In contrast, there are many second class townships with a current tax rate in excess of 30 mills. Those who assume that there is a direct correlation between township class and its tax rate are simply wrong.

The "higher tax" argument for first class townships is at best foolish and, at worst, deliberately deceiving.

Some have asserted that the Pocono First Initiative® simply wants to "get rid of the current board." The motto of Pocono First speaks for itself: "A first class township for a bright future." We are a large bipartisan and diverse group of Pocono Township citizens focused on building a brighter future, not dwelling on the conflict of the past or present. Pocono Township does have problems, but this is all the more reason why we need to move forward and take advantage of a form of government designed to encourage less conflict and better quality governance.

Moving to a first class township is not in the self-interest of supervisors who want to keep their paid jobs or those who stand to benefit from political cronyism, so it is up to the citizens to support equal treatment under the law. Vote "yes" to make Pocono Township first class on November 5th.

We choose to believe in a better future for Pocono Township. It is time to modernize our Township's function, define the roles of those who work on our behalf, and restore transparent decision making done in the general interest of all, not the special interest of a few.[29]—**Judi Coover**

Alongside Judi's editorial was a much shorter, factually flawed and unconvincing argument titled "Solve problems without class change", authored by a resident who opposed the referendum. (Not wishing to embarrass the author, she will be referred to as Mary Smith.)

Solve problems without class change
Editorial by Mary Smith—Pocono Record

As a resident of Pocono Township for the past 27 years and also having been born in Monroe County, I have been following with interest the news articles and letters in support of the First Class Initiative referendum in Pocono Township and their pro's regarding this matter.

Quite frankly, I couldn't fathom there not being any cons or questions regarding this referendum since there are 1,455 second class townships in PA and only 92 first class townships.

I understand what the first class supporters are trying to achieve by opting for a five-member board of supervisors, none of whom would be able to hold a paid township position. The point I wish to make is that there are two second class townships I know of right near us who have five township supervisors on their board and they employ a township manager, zoning officer, SEO, and road master who are not township supervisors. The supervisors may receive a

---

29   Coover, J., "Yes, Pocono residents deserve first class" Pocono Record (9/22/13) http://www.poconorecord.com/apps/pbcs.dll/article?AID=/20130922/NEWS04/309220305

small fee for their time and service capped at $3,000 a year or less.

My question is why is it necessary to change our current system of government under second class to first class, if what we are striving for can be achieved under our current second class status. Also, the millage of a second class township which we currently are is capped at 14 mills.

First class township millage is capped at 30 mills (each of those rates if needed could be raised by petitioning the courts for an additional maximum 5 mills). Are we willing to risk the raising of our millage up to 30 mills? I'm sure right now ours is under 14 mills, but this is something we need to consider.

Another point I'd like to raise is that first class employees, including administrative, public works, and police are classified as Civil Service which opens a whole other can of worms.

Finally, if the referendum for first class status passes, we will have five, yet unknown supervisors, governing our township which would be appointed by a judge to serve until 2015 when the newly elected board would be able to serve. If the reason is driven by anger against the current supervisors, please use the ballot box to elect others.

These are a few of the cons I have discovered. I am in favor of what the residents of the First Class Initiative are trying to change; however, I feel it can be accomplished without jumping into the unknown. If a referendum is needed, why not petition for these changes under second class status?[30]—**Mary Smith**

Ms. Smith was right that there were only 92 first class townships in Pennsylvania compared to 1,455 townships of the second class. In view of that disparity, her inability to *"fathom*

---

[30]   "Solve problems without class change", Pocono Record (9/22/13) http://www.poconorecord.com/apps/pbcs.dll/article?AID=/20130922/ NEWS04/309220304

there not being any cons or questions regarding this referendum" was understandable. It's also easily explained. Since many Pennsylvania townships do not meet the 300 inhabitants per square mile requirement set forth in the First Class Township Code, it's simply a matter of them not being eligible for first class status.

It's also not in the interest of any sitting supervisors in a second class township to move toward first class since they would lose their position as a result of a successful change.

The only way for a second class township to move to first class would be for a grassroots organization on the scale of PFI getting the referendum on the ballot and convincing a majority of voters to vote YES on Election Day.

It would have been prudent for Ms. Smith to carefully fact-check her information before submitting her editorial to the newspaper. She's incorrect about a supervisor salary, and her understanding of tax caps for first and second class townships (correctly stated in Judi's editorial) is erroneous. Her writing loses credibility as a result of her multiple inaccuracies.

Little time was wasted responding to Ms. Smith's editorial. This spirited letter by Maxine Turbolski was published a short time later in the Pocono Record:

Column was wrong on first class move
In Your Opinion—Pocono Record

In response to [Ms. Smith's] Sept. 22 column, "Solve problems without class change": Rather than spending my 300 words pointing out the many factual errors (and there are many) in her writing, I'll focus on her main bone of contention.

[Smith] asks why it's necessary for Pocono Township to change our form of government from second class to first class when what we're striving for can be achieved under our current second-class status.

In answer to her query, I have to say that it's not possible to achieve our goals under our current status. It's not in the interest of the current board of supervisors for our second-class township to go to a five-board format, and it's even less in their interest to prohibit supervisors from holding paid township jobs. In fact, at one of our township meetings, our current supervisor chairman disingenuously expressed an interest in going to five supervisors and we have seen absolutely no effort toward that end. At yet another meeting, he suggested that our township solicitor draw up an ordinance to prohibit supervisors from holding paid township jobs and we have seen no movement toward that goal. And we will not see any action on these matters from our current board, as it would not be in the supervisor's interest.

[Ms. Smith] ends her column by referring to those in favor of the First Class Initiative as "jumping into the unknown." While life is filled with unknowns, I don't believe that becoming a first-class township will have any negative impact. But doing nothing will. Pocono Township has grown, and the old ways of doing township business are no longer effective. It's time to move forward, and becoming a township of the first class is the way to go.[31]— **Maxine Turbolski**

---

[31] Turbolski, M., "Column was wrong on first class move" In Your Opinion, Pocono Record (10/11/13) http://www.poconorecord.com/apps/pbcs.dll/article?AID=/20131011/NEWS04/310110309/-1/NEWS0401

The second of three educational forums on September 24th was a relative success although the turnout was small compared to August 28th. About 50 people attended but that didn't dampen the enthusiasm on the part of PFI. We knew that getting our word out to the community was imperative, no matter how many were listening. We believed that, while 50 was a small number compared to the 150 at our first event, it still indicated an encouraging and continuing interest on the part of residents.

With reporter David Pierce's repeat appearance at the forum, we also knew there would be an informative write-up in the newspaper the next day reaching even more residents. Pierce did not disappoint and Pocono Record readers were kept in the know.

Switch to first class township extolled in Pocono Township
By David Pierce—Pocono Record Writer

Becoming a first class township will create new efficiencies by eliminating supervisor preoccupation and infighting over self-appointed jobs, 50 Pocono Township residents were told during a forum Tuesday night.

Several speakers representing Pocono First Initiative—a political action committee that petitioned for a November voter referendum to change the township's governance—emphasized that belief repeatedly.

Pocono is currently a second class township with three elected supervisors who can and do appoint themselves to township jobs. If the referendum wins voter approval, they would be replaced by five commissioners who are prohibited by state code from holding township employment.

"Going to a first class township is not more big government," said Taylor Munoz, asserting the change will weed out candidates who are looking for work.

Many second class supervisors are unqualified for their self-appointed jobs, Jack Swersie said.

"It also can lead to infighting among supervisors looking for jobs," Swersie said. "They become their own bosses. They sign their own paychecks."

A three-member panel was asked if five good commissioner candidates could be found in Pocono Township willing to take the position for $3,250 each.

"Again, these are people who are not interested in jobs," Scott Gilliland said. "They're interested in a format where they might be able to make a difference."

Speakers said that increasing the number of elected supervisors from three to five—without becoming a first class township—wouldn't end self-appointed jobs. They said first class commissioners would be more responsive to voters because they serve four-year terms, compared to six-year supervisor terms.

One resident asked why there are only 92 first class townships, compared to 1,455 second class townships, if going first class is such a good idea.

Munoz said the state code requires a voter referendum petition to become first class, something supervisors don't want.

"It's not in their interest to necessarily support a measure on the ballot that could lose them their jobs," Munoz said.

Townships must achieve a population density of at least 300 people per square mile before becoming first class, he added.

It took a monumental effort to collect the minimum 5 percent of township voter signatures to get the proposal on the ballot, Judi Coover said.

"It takes a lot of work," she said. "Twenty of us have been working since February. We spent our own money."

First Initiative panelists also refuted claims that becoming a first class township would trigger tax hikes.[32]—**David Pierce**

---

[32]   Pierce, D., "Switch to first class township extolled in Pocono Township" Pocono Record (9/25/13) http://www.poconorecord.com/apps/pbcs.dll/ article?AID=/20130925/NEWS/309250332/-1/rss01

There were only about five weeks left until the election. While CCPT had indicated to PFI on several occasions that they saw the passage of first class as inevitable and would not fight it, there were those within their organization who were still on the fence. Inside talk was that they needed to decide their official position and take a stand. A September 26th meeting was called. It would be held at a business location owned by a CCPT member and would be attended by about two dozen others.

Judi and Taylor were invited. Say's Judi, "*They seemed to want a face to face open discussion to see if we were truly convinced and sincere about first class.*"

The two arrived at the meeting armed with a presentation aimed at unequivocally convincing CCPT that first class was the best option for Pocono Township. But they were unable to complete their talk. Five minutes after they began extolling the benefits of first class, they were bombarded with a litany of questions. Most were straight forward and quickly answered by Judi or Taylor. A few questions were more probing and aggressive but Taylor recalls that "*overall, it was not a hostile environment and there were some good questions asked.*"

After about an hour, the question/answer session was over and Judi and Taylor left the meeting. While they were standing in the parking lot talking to each other, the meeting inside had ended and CCPT members began to leave the building. One attendee told them that the group had taken a vote before they ended their meeting and that at least one-half to two-thirds of their members were now in favor of first class.

It appeared as though Judi and Taylor had made their case, but we would soon see that appearances can be quite deceiving.

CHAPTER 18
OCTOBER SURPRISES

October before the election, probably the most important month of a political campaign, could not have been any more troublesome for the majority supervisors. A controversial proposal regarding the replacement of Central Pocono Ambulance Association, more smoke-screen suggestions, alleged zoning violations by a business owned by the Hess family and a township educational forum promised to be unbiased would lead to negative press coverage and a level of distrust that cannot be overstated.

PFI stayed their course, making the case to those in the community still unsure of which direction would best suit the township. We continued to maintain a cautious optimism.

As a successful businessman, Frank Hess most likely would have had his eye on minimizing expenses to increase his business's bottom line. Now, as a politician his focus seemed to be on cutting taxes for his constituents by minimizing township expenses. The BOS had already eliminated full-time township positions such as Zoning Officer and Sewage Enforcement Officer, outsourcing those responsibilities to part-time professionals. No one argued with those bold and effective moves.

But Hess's proposal to replace Central Pocono Ambulance as the township's primary emergency responder and potentially save taxpayers $140,000 in annual subsidies[33] deeply disturbed residents. Pocono Central had served the township for over 50 years and the quality of service they provided was exemplary.

---

[33]   Pierce, D., "Pocono Township weighs ambulance options" Pocono Record (10/7/13) http://www.poconorecord.com/apps/pbcs.dll/article?AID=/20131007/NEWS/310070319

Few people were convinced that a change would be in the best interest of the township.

Whether Hess was using Pocono Central *"in an attempt to get back at Jane Cilurso"* as Roy Smith and others believed or whether he sincerely felt he could save taxpayer money while still providing the same level of service was something only he knew for certain. Unfortunately for him, many people believed the former.

Many also believed that, for him, cutting taxes had become a campaign strategy to oppose first class. As the election drew near, it looked as though he was making a final effort to save his administration by showing residents he was saving them money.

The tax-cutting theme continued.

According to the Second Class Township Code it was imperative for the BOS to adopt a final budget not later than the last day of December.[34] The supervisors had been working on the township's 2014 budget behind closed doors and Hess had been hinting for at least a month that there would be a 2-mill local tax reduction for the following year. (Millage rate is the amount per $1,000 that is used to calculate taxes on property. A 2-mill reduction in Pocono Township would amount to an average of $60 per taxpayer.) It was suspect that the positive budget presentation was only aimed at defeating the first class referendum. After all, *"the budget was scheduled for tentative adoption on November 4th, the night before the municipal elections when township voters would consider replacing Pocono's second class township governance."*[35]

Because the BOS were not openly working on the budget, residents wanted the supervisors to hold a public workshop so they could see the proposed budget for themselves and make comments and suggestions where necessary. Under much

---

[34] Second Class Township Code, Pennsylvania State Association of Township Supervisors Website: http://www.psats.org/subpage.php?pageid=secondclasstownshipcode

[35] Pierce, D., "Supervisors eye possible tax decrease" Pocono Record (10/30/13) http://www.poconorecord.com/apps/pbcs.dll/article?AID=/20131030/NEWS/310300335/-1/news

pressure the BOS agreed to a meeting to review the budget at the end of October.

At the heavily-attended workshop the township administrator presented the budget complete with its proposed tax cut, stating that *"the final numbers could change."*

Implying that the announcement of a tax decrease was politically motivated, PFI's Scott Gilliland asked; *"Why announce two weeks ahead of time a two mill reduction when there might not be a reduction in the final budget?"*[36]

Noting that only $300,000 was budgeted for roads in 2014, Judi and Werkheiser argued with Hess and Bengel that it wasn't enough money to maintain the 80-plus miles of township roads. Werkheiser said it costs $100,000 per mile to tar and chip roads and by properly maintaining them in that manner, the life of each road is greatly extended. In the long run, that saves the township money. With $300,000 budgeted for road work, only three miles of roads could be properly maintained in 2014. Many residents at the workshop agreed that they would prefer not to have a $60 tax decrease, if the alternative was having better roads on which to drive.

Hess said he would *"take it under advisement,"* the workshop was adjourned and residents left, believing that the announcement of a 2-mill tax cut was not at all genuine and that the chairman knew it would have to be reversed at some point after the election.

Pocono Record's David Pierce, in an early October article, observed, *"Pocono Township Supervisor Frank Hess hopes to head off a voter referendum to change the township's governance by eliminating self-appointed township jobs for supervisors."*[37]

It was apparent what the motivation was when the BOS voted to have the township solicitor draft a resolution to that

---

[36]   Pierce, D., "Supervisors eye possible tax decrease" Pocono Record (10/30/13) http://www.poconorecord.com/apps/pbcs.dll/ article?AID=/20131030/NEWS/310300335/-1/news

[37]   Pierce, D., "Pocono Township supervisor: Take away my job" Pocono Record (10/11/13) http://www.poconorecord.com/apps/pbcs.dll/ article?AID=/20131011/NEWS/310110330/-1/NEWSLETTER100

effect. They planned to pass the resolution at the next township meeting which would fall on October 21st, fifteen days before Election Day. From a strategic standpoint their timing might very well have been perfect.

Two weeks later however, our own township solicitor said, *"If passed, the resolution could easily be reversed, making it little more than a symbolic measure."*[38] Two disappointed supervisors along with Werkheiser then voted to table the proposal and that would be the last we would hear of it.

This Pocono Record headline could not have come at a worse time for Chairman Hess: *"Pocono Township supervisor's son in zoning fight. Rival fuel companies bicker over business operations; favoritism alleged."*[39]

According to David Pierce, Furino Fuels, owned by Hess's step-son, had been cited for four zoning violations for allegedly running a fuel business at their home property which was zoned residential. According to the Notice of Violation by the township part-time zoning officer, *"the zoning permit clearly states the garage is to be used for residential purposes only. However it appears that you are operating a vehicle service and repair facility, which is only permitted in a commercial zone as specified in the Pocono Township zoning ordinance use schedule."*[40]

The complaint against Furino Fuels was initiated by a local competitor who claimed they had made five unsuccessful visits to the township demanding an inspection of the Furino property. They suggested that the supervisor chairman may have prevented the zoning officer from doing the inspection earlier.

Whether or not the allegations against Furino Fuels and Hess would be proven true would be determined at a later hearing

---

38   Reber, C., "Pocono Supervisors can't ban themselves from paid jobs" Pocono Record (10/22/13) http://www.poconorecord.com/apps/pbcs.dll/article?AID=/20131022/NEWS/131029929

39   Pierce, D. "Pocono Township supervisor's son in zoning fight" Pocono Record (10/14/13) http://www.poconorecord.com/apps/pbcs.dll/article?AID=/20131014/NEWS/310140312/-1/NEWSLETTER100

40   Pierce, D. "Pocono Township supervisor's son in zoning fight" Pocono Record (10/14/13) http://www.poconorecord.com/apps/pbcs.dll/article?AID=/20131014/NEWS/310140312/-1/NEWSLETTER100

before the Zoning Board, but it didn't matter on October 14th when the article was published. The damage had been done. It was very bad publicity for the chairman.

Both father and step-son had strong feelings about the alleged violations.

"I believe some of the competitors located in Pocono Township are not pleased that my business has affected their bottom line or the fact that my father, Frank J. Hess Sr., is a Pocono Township supervisor," Furino contends. *"Since they cannot prevail in a professional manner, they decided to attack my family and myself personally."*

Hess added, *"Some people know how to use the system, use the system to eliminate competition."*[41]

Nothing seemed to go Hess's way in October. This strongly worded letter to the editor by Linda Kresge added fuel to his fire.

Replace Pocono dictators with first class status
In Your Opinion—Pocono Record

The foundations of our democracy are based on accountability in government, public engagement and elected leaders who represent the best interests of citizens. But Pocono Township residents receive none of these. They are not being governed, they are being ruled.

Pocono Township officials are no longer accountable. Public workshops have been abolished, quashing the opportunity for the public to voice important concerns and opinions. Those who simply attend regular meetings see the grievous effects of the supervisor's lack of facts and intelligible answers to public questions. Decisions that are made are either done in haste—regularly claiming that the issue at hand is "an emergency"—or done behind

41   Pierce, D. "Pocono Township supervisor's son in zoning fight" Pocono Record (10/14/13) http://www.poconorecord.com/apps/pbcs.dll/article?AID=/20131014/NEWS/310140312/-1/NEWSLETTER100

closed doors, thereby disregarding the state's Sunshine Law.

Examples of Pocono Township's less-than-exemplary decision-making include: removing a sitting road master under false pretenses and replacing him with an advertising salesman; the mysterious shifting around of monies between budget line items; requiring right-to-know forms five days in advance for all information; refusing to address a formal complaint that a supervisor's son is operating a commercial enterprise in a residential zone without required permits. Also the township's out-of-date zoning ordinances, no plan for road maintenance and high sewer fees that will severely impact Route 611 property owners.

The 2014 budget continues to be kept under wraps, with no official date set for a public workshop, and the proposed budget will effectively defund and eliminate the nonprofit Central Pocono Ambulance. In all likelihood, there will be no public input.

Majority Chairman Frank Hess continues to make these decisions unilaterally with the township administrator, who was hired without public input, without a contract and without a job description. Oh yeah, and he's from Bucks County, and does not live or pay taxes here.

Sounds like a dictatorship to me. Vote first class in November.[42]—**Linda Kresge**

Every proposal and decision made by the majority supervisors was questioned by those closely watching. An argument could be made that many of their actions lacked transparency and fairness and were made only for the sake of political expediency.

---

[42] Kresge, L., "Replace Pocono dictators with first class status" In Your Opinion, Pocono Record (10/11/13) http://www.poconorecord.com/apps/pbcs.dll/article?AID=/20131011/NEWS04/310110308/-1/NEWSLETTER100

That was no way to run a township.

Fifty yard signs strategically placed in Pocono Township by PFI.

The third and final PFI educational forum was presented at Northampton Community College on the evening of October 24th. Attendance was modest compared to the first event back in late August but better than the September turnout. The election was twelve days away and, while no one in PFI was overconfident, the general feeling was positive.

Like our previous forums we allowed three of our team members a few minutes to express their conviction for first class. Diane, Debra and I took to the podium with our impassioned views.

Debra led the way.

"Good evening everyone. My name is Debra Morrishow. I grew up in New York and now I live in Tannersville. I love living in the Poconos. I've been living here for 3 years. I may be new to the Poconos but I'm not new to how things work in a community. I served on Community Board 10 in New York and I'm presently a board member of my homeowners association.

Back in 2012, I started attending the township meetings. I came home from the first meeting and told my husband, I think the guys in charge are in over their head.

Over the years I've gotten to know the 3 supervisors and they seem like nice guys. But I feel because of the size of our township it would make better sense to have a different form of government.

Having 5 commissioners being paid $3,250 a year will free up funds to hire the professionals we need to properly run our township. Our present system allows our supervisors to appoint themselves to a position even if they are not qualified for the position.

I will admit that I like walking into the township office and being able to talk directly to a supervisor when I have an issue. Some people may think that if we become a first class township that there will be no one in the office who is in charge. That is not true. Our township can have a township manager who will be in charge and who will report to the commissioners.

Also, a township manager in a first class township can operate more autonomously and objectively than in a second-class township, since his or her employment does not depend on two majority supervisors (as in a second class township).

I would like you to think about these questions:

Do you feel that our large township can be properly run by 3 supervisors? If your answer is NO then you should vote YES to Pocono Township becoming first class.

And ask yourself; is it okay for supervisors to appoint themselves to paying jobs even if they are not qualified? If your answer is NO then you should vote YES to Pocono Township becoming first class.

I invite everyone to attend the next Board of Supervisors meeting to see how our government presently operates. It will be Nov. 4 at 7pm at the Municipal Building."—**Debra Morrishow**

As the enthusiastic applause for Debra's thoughts and words quieted, I stepped up to share mine.

"Thank you all for being here tonight. My name is Jack Swersie. I've been a Pocono Township resident for 26 years and I've been going to our township meetings for the past three or four.

When I first heard about the Pocono First Initiative, I went online and downloaded the Pennsylvania First Class Township Code and the Pennsylvania Township Commissioners Handbook. I've read through both and I am convinced that First Class is the way to go forward in Pocono Township.

Under our current Second Class status we have three elected supervisors who, in most cases, appoint themselves to paid township jobs. While that is legal under the second class code, I don't think it's a good idea. And while there are other issues, that's the main one that convinced me to support the First Class Initiative.

The ability for a supervisor to appoint him or herself to a paid township job can lead to situations where people run for office simply to access a full-time job whether they are qualified for that job or not. It can also lead to in-fighting among those jockeying for a particular job and that wastes valuable time and resources. None of this is fair to us taxpayers who foot the bill.

When elected leaders work for the township, there are no checks and balances. No oversight. They become their own boss. They sign their own paychecks. Mistakes or misdeeds can go unchecked. That can create mistrust and a governing body cannot effectively govern if they've lost the trust of their constituents.

We need to have leaders who are legislators, not administrators. We want them to have the energy and focus to make policy to plan for the future of our growing township. We don't need them to be bogged down with the day to day administrative duties for which in many cases they have no professional experience.

It has been proposed by our board of supervisors that we can achieve the same results within the structure of second class by simply passing a resolution prohibiting supervisors from taking paid township jobs. As simple as that might sound, it specifically states in the Township Supervisors Handbook that resolutions have no force or effect of law. That means a resolution does NOT, and can NOT, legally change Pennsylvania code. Even our township lawyer stated at Monday night's meeting that a resolution can NOT bind future supervisor boards and that it would be equally simple for future supervisors to pass yet another resolution overturning the prohibition and bringing things back to business as usual. I don't think we need, nor do I think we want, business as usual in Pocono Township.

Under the Pennsylvania first class code, it is set in stone that elected leaders cannot hold paid township jobs. That law, like all township governing laws, can NOT be changed based on political or personal expediency.

First class is the way to go forward and I ask that you vote YES on November 5th."—**Jack Swersie**

Diane, who unlike Debra and I, had not expressed her views at previous forums followed us and hit the ball out of the park.

"My name is Diane Zweifel. I was born, raised and educated in New York City. I have lived in Pocono Township since the 1970s.

Back then I was young and naïve about local government. When there would be an upcoming supervisor election, I would think, "that's unimportant, I don't have to waste time voting in that election!"

It took a while but I soon learned how wrong I was. It is THAT level of government (local government) that has the most direct influence over your day-to-day activities. Local elected officials can pass an ordinance one day that we would have to abide by the next day in order to comply with the law.

Over the years, I sporadically attended township meetings and I became very frustrated. I thought I couldn't make much of a difference by expressing my concerns about issues that were important to me and my husband. The supervisors would listen, say they "would look into things" and then nothing much ever changed.

I started attending township meetings more regularly last year, and yes there were still times of frustration, but there also seemed to be a few more people expressing their concerns about the way things were and I began to see a glimmer of hope in changing the "politics as usual."

I am astonished that a group of 20 or so people can get together, work together in a relatively short period of time, research what they feel is a better form of government, fund the effort out of their own pockets and potentially accomplish a change in their form of local government. I am proud to be part of this group—Pocono First Initiative. I feel that elevating to First Class—having 5 Commissioners who cannot, by law, sign their own pay checks, limiting terms to 4 years and having more transparency in our government—will be a great thing.

Hopefully, people will come out to vote on November 5th. There are approximately 7,500 registered voters in Pocono Township and just about 1,300 of them voted in the last municipal election. The fact that you are in this audience tells me that you are among that 1,300. So please VOTE YES to elevate Pocono Township to a First Class Township. Thank you."—**Diane Zweifel**

Lower Macungie Township Commissioner's President Ron Eichenberg was our featured speaker. He painted a clear and convincing picture of the transparency and efficiency found in his own first class governed township, leaving few in the room in doubt that it truly was the way to go forward in Pocono Township.

In an October 26ᵗʰ Pocono Record article titled "Pocono Township has questions about first class status," David Pierce captured the evening's conversation.

Pocono Township has questions about first class status
By David Pierce—Pocono Record Writer

It isn't clear what process Monroe County Court would use to select temporary commissioners if Pocono Township voters agree Nov. 5 to become a first class township, those attending a public forum were told Thursday night.

Township voters are being asked if they want to replace the second class township governance of three elected supervisors, each serving six-year terms, with a first class township of five elected commissioners, each serving four-year terms.

If the referendum is approved, Monroe County Court will name five temporary commissioners to serve during a two-year transition leading to new elections.

In Lower Macungie Township, where voters agreed in 2007 to convert to first class, all Lehigh County judges reviewed applications and voted privately on a slate of temporary commissioners.

"We don't know what our court will do," said Judi Coover of Pocono First Initiative, the group that circulated a petition to put the first class question before voters in Pocono Township.

State law places the temporary appointments in the court's hands but doesn't specify the process.

Pocono First Initiative has asked Monroe County Court if procedures are being developed, Coover said, but hasn't yet received an answer.

The selection procedure was one of several written questions put to a Pocono First Initiative panel during the forum at Northampton Community College's Tannersville campus.

Lower Macungie Commissioners President Ron Eichenberg said his township's decision to convert to first class has resulted in a more transparent and efficient government, while maintaining its zero municipal property tax rate.

A group similar to Pocono First Initiative launched the Lower Macungie referendum drive after a second class township supervisor embezzled $2 million from the township sewer fund, he said.

"Six years ago, we were where you are today," Eichenberg said. "Back then, people just didn't miss $2 million. That was our impetus back then to go from second class to first class."

Once it was approved, Lehigh County judges selected a talented, but diverse group that included an attorney, engineer, accountant and a planner, he said. They paved the way for elections two years later to staggered four-year township commissioner terms.

Now elected township officials focus on legislative matters, with a township manager overseeing a professional working staff, he said.

Though second class supervisors can appoint themselves to township jobs, state law prohibits first class commissioners from taking paid township jobs.

Eichenberg, as board president, and the township manager jointly sign all checks. Eichenberg scrutinizes expenditures and will call the finance director if he has questions, he said.

"There is total transparency in a first class township," Eichenberg said.[43]—**David Pierce**

---

[43]   Pierce, D., "Pocono Township has questions about first class status" Pocono Record (10/26/13) http://www.poconorecord.com/apps/pbcs.dll/article?AID=/20131026/NEWS/310260341/-1/rss01

PFI's forums were now in the past but there would still be one more educational event.

Frank Hess had been promoting his upcoming BOS educational forum as strictly informational and balanced, implying that ours were biased toward first class. But our events were never intended to do anything but educate the public on why we were convinced that first class was the best way forward. We had been up front about that from day one. Residents were living and breathing the downside of second class governance and came to our events to learn how the first class structure might better suit the needs of Pocono Township.

The BOS forum, two days after PFI's last, would prove to be biased before anyone even walked through the door.

The clock ticked toward Election Day.

One evening, Judi received a phone call from a CCPT member who advised her that their group had decided to take a formal stance against our initiative. This announcement didn't come as a surprise to PFI. We did find it puzzling that they would choose to formally let us know of their decision, but we were glad they did.

We were now bracing for an array of negative campaigning, unaware of just how overwhelming it would be. In anticipation of what was to come, PFI moved forward with our usual focus and determination.

A huge promotional mailing had already been planned and postcards would soon make their way to over 3,500 Pocono Township homes. We would use the U. S. Post Office direct mail option in an attempt to reach every household with our township zip code. The plan was to have the postcards arrive in mailboxes on the Saturday and Monday before the Tuesday election. Timing would be of the utmost importance.

We also started our telephone campaign. Using phone lists containing the numbers of those who had voted in the last several elections, team members spent hours each evening talking to fellow residents. It's estimated that PFI made close to 1,000 phone calls prior to the election. While there were those who would rudely hang up on us, the general response we received from those with whom we spoke was positive.

Diane continued her letter to the editor coordination and the Pocono Record continued to print submissions by residents.

PFI thought it important to remind voters of who was supporting the first class referendum and who was trying to have it silenced. The publication of this concise and to-the-point letter could not have been better timed:

Don't settle for biz as usual in Pocono
In Your Opinion—Pocono Record

When a nonpartisan grassroots group of Pocono Township residents tirelessly work to get a referendum on the ballot and then feverishly push to see it pass, it's because they see something in their local government not working the way it should and sincerely believe there's a better way forward. Such is the selfless story of the Pocono First Initiative.

When a small but vocal opposition emerges, one should take a good look at those behind that movement and ask what their motivation might be. As citizens of our township, they surely have their concerns. But are those concerns altruistic or a desire to maintain their own political power and influence?

Voting YES for first class will provide a fresh approach to governing Pocono Township. The alternative is business as usual.

Vote YES for first class![44]—**Jack Swersie**

PFI was keeping all eyes on the finish line and so too was the opposition. While they had continuously tried to have us believe they would be taking a back seat to the passage of the referendum, no one on our team ever believed that they would not put up a fight. After their recent announcement that they would officially counter our efforts, we expected that fight to be very aggressive. That would turn out to be an understatement.

It would all begin on October 30th at the BOS educational forum.

44   Swersie, J., "Don't settle for biz as usual in Pocono" In Your Opinion, Pocono Record (10/25/13) http://www.poconorecord.com/apps/pbcs.dll/article?AID=/20131025/NEWS04/310250339/-1/rss31

CHAPTER 21

THE BOS EDUCATIONAL FORUM

It was six days before the election. For several weeks, Hess had been promoting the BOS forum as being one which would extoll the virtues and reveal the cons of both first and second class townships.

"Unbiased!" he loudly and proudly proclaimed.

The plan was to present two attorneys from the Bucks County law firm of Grim, Biehn and Thatcher, both with extensive experience in municipal law, to provide information on the two different governing structures. Hess said that the attorneys would be doing this presentation pro-bono.

Why he would be using a Bucks County law firm and why attorneys would be providing their expertise at no charge were two questions on everyone's mind and prompted an investigation by PFI.

Monica discovered that Grim, Biehn and Thatcher was the law firm currently representing Pocono Township for an ongoing dispute involving the township's newly installed sewer line and that $97,000 had been paid to them over the course of the last year. Additional research revealed that our township administrator just happened to be the best friend of that law firm's managing partner. He had been quoted as referring to the managing partner as *"like a brother to me."*[45]

Unbiased? It was understandable why, days before the forum even took place, people were becoming increasingly skeptical.

Skepticism turned to outright anger the night of the forum. Upon walking into the meeting hall at St. Paul Lutheran Church in Tannersville, attendees were provided with a fact sheet put

---

[45] Plumstead Watchdogs Website:
    http://plumsteadwatchdogs.blogspot.com/2010/01/what-is-really-going-on-in-plumstead_15.html

together by Grim, Biehn and Thatcher and a two-sided, 8 ½" x 5 ½", anti-first class postcard produced by CCPT. That was just the beginning of their literary campaign of half-truths and misinformation that would flood the township until Election Day.

Judging by attendance, this event was an undeniable success. But while there were those still unsure about first class, the majority of attendees appeared to be supporters of the referendum. After staying away from all three PFI educational forums, members of CCPT were now heavily represented, sitting together on one side of the room while PFI sat mostly on the other side.

Waiting for the forum to begin, supporters of the referendum sat in utter disbelief, stunned by the fact that Hess would allow CCPT to distribute anti-first class literature at this event. It showed a blatant disregard for his own promise of an unbiased forum and further eroded public trust toward both Hess and CCPT.

Each side of the postcard provided by CCPT said pretty much the same thing. One side presented their argument from the standpoint of why one should vote NO, how a NO vote would allow Pocono Township to remain second class, and why that would be a good idea. The other side tells the reader to "PLEASE VOTE WISELY AND KNOW WHAT IT MEANS TO VOTE NO." Both sides of the postcard approached the same issues but from a different angle and showed either a lack of understanding of what changing to first class would mean or a purposeful attempt at deception.

CHANGING TO A FIRST CLASS TOWNSHIP MEANS:

Raises the general purpose tax rate to 30mils.

Mandates that all future police officers hired qualify as Civil Servants.

Mandates a Township Manager Position.

Substitutes elected Supervisors with Court Appointed Commissioners.

Mandates that anyone holding a position with the township must quit their job before they can seek public office.

Can result with 5 new commissioners who have no experience running the township and potentially no experience with the sewer system and its known deficiencies.

Six questionable assertions on postcard distributed by CCPT.

It's easy to strike down each of the six points listed under "CHANGING TO A FIRST CLASS TOWNSHIP MEANS:"

(1) *"Raises the maximum general purpose tax rate to 30 mils."* This statement is very deceptive. Yes, the general millage rate is 30 in first class townships as opposed to 14 in second class. But that's completely ignoring the second class allowable millage rates for ambulance and rescue squads, road equipment, fire hydrants, and street lights. All told, when added together, the millage rate has a higher cap in second class.

(2) *"Mandates that all future police officers hired qualify as Civil Servants."* It's true that all officers hired in the future would have to pass a Civil Service exam in order to qualify but setting standards for employment would help maintain a high level of performance.

(3) *"Mandates a township manager position."* It's quite obvious that CCPT did not read the Pennsylvania First Class Township Code. Nowhere in the code does it mandate the hiring

84

of a township manager. Instead, the code gives commissioners the right "to create, by ordinance, the office of township manager, and in like manner to abolish the same."[46] It's no different than in a second class township.

(4) **"Substitutes elected supervisors with court appointed commissioners."** Yes, should our township become one of the first class, the current BOS would be abolished and judges would select an interim board of five commissioners who would serve for only two years. At the next municipal election voters would once again decide who their leaders would be. CCPT was trying to make it appear that residents would forever lose their right to vote if first class passed. That statement is a blatant stretch of the truth.

(5) **"Mandates that anyone holding a position with the township must quit their job before they can seek public office."** Nowhere in the First Class Township Code is that stated.

(6) **"Can result with 5 new commissioners who have no experience running the township and potentially no experience with the sewer system and its known deficiencies."** This is a scare-tactic. Any time new officials are elected there's a learning curve. That's the chance we take whenever we vote for new leaders. Since the court would be appointing interim commissioners, we should feel confident that the judges would select the most qualified applicants. With regard to the sewer system, the current BOS had been in charge for over two years and those *"known deficiencies"* still existed.

Confusion and deception was what it was all about. That seemed to be their game plan. This piece of literature should have been an unequivocal embarrassment to all those associated with CCPT. Instead it would serve as the foundation for what they would expound as truth from forum day until Election Day, even after the attorney from Grim, Biehn and Thatcher debunked each and every point.

---

[46]   PA. State Legislature website, First Class Township Code: http://www. legis.state.pa.us/WU01/LI/LI/US/HTM/1931/0/0331. HTM

Contrary to what we were told to expect, when the forum began there was only one attorney and PFI attendees braced themselves for what they expected to be a pro-second class lecture. Thankfully that was not the case.

According to his profile on the Grim, Biehn & Thatcher website, John B. Rice is a highly experienced attorney who concentrates his legal practice in the areas of municipal law, zoning and land use and eminent domain law. His experience includes over 25 years of service to municipalities, municipal authorities, citizens groups and individual clients. He has litigated land use, environmental, and regulatory issues before local and state administrative agencies. His dedication and commitment provide both municipalities and individual clients a diverse range of solutions in the field of municipal law.[47]

Attorney Rice could not have been a more objective speaker and people's worries in that regard were quickly put to rest. He began his presentation by introducing himself and describing his professional background as well as that of his law firm. Then, referring to the fact sheet he provided, he walked residents step by step through the structural differences between first and second class; supervisors versus commissioners, six year terms versus four years, eligibility for township employment and health insurance, civil service requirements for police in first and second class, and elected and appointed officers required in each class.

Continuing his impartial presentation, he carefully explained the procedure that would be followed should the first class referendum pass. He explained that the current supervisors, the tax collector and the auditors would lose their positions effective the first Monday of January, 2014 and that the Monroe County Court of Common Pleas would appoint five commissioners, a tax collector and three auditors to replace the governing board. Those transitional court appointed officials would hold office for two years, after which new officers would be voted in by residents.

Most importantly, Rice went on to describe in detail the tax structure in a first class township compared to that of second

---

[47] Grim, Biehn & Thatcher Website: http://www.grimlaw.com/
      attorney-profiles/john-b-rice

class. He made it clear that, while the "general purpose" millage cap was 30 in a first class township versus 14 in second class, when one includes the "special purpose" rates, the total millage rate cap is actually higher in second class than in first class. That clearly contradicted CCPT's assertion that taxes could and would increase in a first class township. Of course, that fact would be conveniently ignored by the determined opposition.

Following Rice's presentation, a question and answer session brought residents from both sides of the aisle up to the microphone. Over the next hour the attorney objectively answered questions, eventually striking down all of the assertions made by CCPT in their anti-first class literature.

The bias that Hess infused into the BOS forum by allowing CCPT to distribute their postcard, when all was said and done, did not define the entire evening. Any reasonable and objective observer would have concluded that the attorney's involvement in the proceedings allowed for a fair-minded look at first class versus second, one that was free of bias and very informative and one that would do little to dissuade voters from voting YES.

Encapsulating the forum in the next day's Pocono Record, David Pierce wrote the following:

Merits of first class reviewed in Pocono Township
By David Pierce—Pocono Record Writer

If Pocono Township becomes a first class township, police officers will be subject to civil service regulations overseen by an appointed commission, a municipal attorney said at a public forum Wednesday.

The three-member volunteer civil service commission, advised by a paid attorney, would set rules and regulations for hiring, firing and promoting officers on Pocono's 17-member force, Bucks County attorney John Rice said.

He believes current pay and benefits of the township officers wouldn't change as a result of changing from a second class to a first class township.

Rice made a presentation and took questions from more than 75 people at the forum arranged by Pocono Township Supervisors Chairman Frank Hess.

A group of residents successfully petitioned for a voter referendum that, if approved by township voters Tuesday, will require the township to replace its three elected supervisors, each serving six-year terms, with five elected commissioners serving four-year terms.

If approved, Monroe County Court would appoint temporary commissioners to serve during a two-year transition to new elections.

Members of First Class Initiative, which initiated the petition drive, point to a first class ban on elected officials holding paid township jobs as a major reason to make the change. Two of Pocono Township's second class supervisors currently hold township jobs.

Second class townships traditionally had small populations, no zoning ordinances and few supervisor responsibilities beyond paving and plowing roads, Rice said. To do this, a supervisor would take a paid job as a road master.

"That's the reason for the employment provision in a second class township," Rice said.

But Rice doubts there is a difference between the type of government a township has and how well the township is operated.

"You've got to have the right people in office asking the right questions," he said. "I'm here to tell you, with your form of government, if you don't have the right people, it doesn't matter."

Attendees were allowed to ask one question each of Rice.

Some Pocono First Initiative members charged the forum was biased in favor of those who want to keep Pocono's current form of governance, contrary to assertions by Hess that it was strictly informational.

Pocono First Initiative member Monica Gerrity said she found out through a public records request that Rice's law firm was paid $97,000 by Pocono Township during the past year. Most of that was for representing the township in litigating responsibility for fixing a flawed township sewer line.

Grim, Biehn and Thatcher represent first and second class townships, boroughs and home rule municipalities throughout eastern Pennsylvania, Rice said. His representation of Pocono had no impact on his presentation, Rice said.

"I don't have a horse in this race," Rice said. "I'm very busy with what I'm doing, whether it's Pocono or something else." He said anti-referendum literature in the Pocono Lutheran Church auditorium authored by the "Concerned Citizens of Pocono Township Pennsylvania Association" wasn't placed there by him.

Though many have taken sides, some residents said they remain undecided on the referendum.[48]— **David Pierce**

---

[48] Pierce, D. "Merits of first class reviewed in Pocono Township" Pocono Record (11/1/13) http://www.poconorecord.com/apps/pbcs.dll/article?AID=/20131101/NEWS/311010335

Immediately after the BOS educational forum, it became clear that CCPT was prepared to heavily invest in their campaign to derail the first class referendum in the last days before the election.

We had assumed that, as part of their recently announced formal opposition to first class, they would send mailers, make phone calls and post signs but we had no way to know how incredibly fervent their efforts would be. The next six days would see them mount an even more powerful and aggressive fight using the same talking points shown by Attorney Rice to be false. It appeared to mean nothing to the group that the information they were disseminating was at best misleading and at worst, untrue. And spending large sums of money was no objective for them when it came to getting out their message of "VOTE NO TO FIRST CLASS!"

PFI was holding firm in their belief that CCPT had grossly underestimated the intelligence of our fellow residents and that the voters would see through their desperate, last minute, win-at-all-cost campaign of misinformation, half-truths and deception. We would soon know for sure if that was to be.

CCPT's final campaign began with an ad. Relatively speaking it was a small one, only a quarter of a page in the Pocono Record and running through the weekend of November 1st. Over the next few days, we would see that it was only a modest first step of a negative publicity blitz by the opposition. The ad, containing the usual blather, was inconspicuously buried within the newspaper and could very well have been overlooked by readers.

In sharp contrast to the weekend newspaper ads were the intermittent ones illuminating the two giant digital billboards along Route 611, the main highway through Pocono Township. Appearing every two minutes, sandwiched between more traditional billboard ads, one would have needed more than eight seconds to fully read each of the two different ads by CCPT. But the message was very clear on both: "VOTE NO!"

Potentially more damaging to the passage of the referendum was the online Pocono Record ad, again purchased by CCPT, which consisted of a "drop-down" banner atop the front page. All one had to do was run their mouse curser over the banner and a huge ad dropped down, covering half of the computer screen. There was nothing new in the ad, but it allowed the reader more viewing time than the digital billboards allowed and it was more easily noticed than the quarter page ad buried deep within the newspaper. This drop-down ad remained on the front page of the online paper throughout the weekend and was a constant reminder that CCPT would spare no expense and say whatever they needed to say in order to see first class fail.

It looked like the opposition had the same idea as we did and on November 1st when we mailed 3,500 postcards promoting first class, they made a similar move with their message of "NO." Our postcards were mailed using the U.S. Post Office direct mail option which allowed us to reach every address in the township at a fraction of the cost of other mailing options. It is believed that CCPT used a "super voter" list to target only those with a proven track record of voting in local elections and with that they may have been able to reach about 1,000 voters.

They used the same 8 ½" x 5 ½" postcard distributed at the BOS forum to send to the super voters. What PFI would eventually save on postage cost had been used to create a larger and more visually striking postcard, simply written, bold in its design and appearing more professional than the opposition's card. Timed by both groups to find their way into mailboxes on the Saturday and Monday before the election, the two postcards would compete for attention. Our colorful 12" x 6" postcard would surely catch the eye of the recipient first, while CCPT's might very well get lost in a pile of mail.

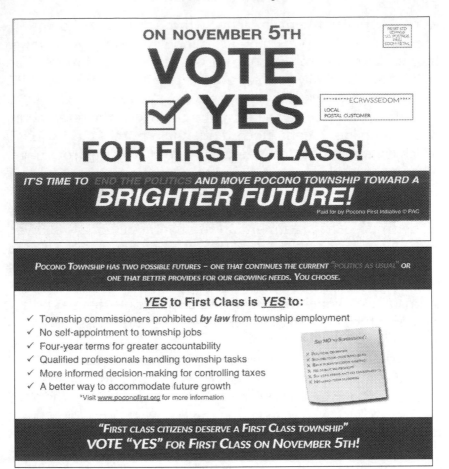

PFI's visually striking two-sided postcard.

Simply written, bold in design and mailed to 3,500 residents.

There was little that PFI could do to counter the last-minute, heavy-handed, anti-referendum storm and everyone within the group was growing frustrated and concerned. From the start of our initiative, we all believed that travelling the high road throughout the process, as we had been doing, would be the key to our ultimate success and we continued along that path. We knew that our last line of defense against CCPT's loud and desperate cries would be at the polls on Election Day.

Before sunrise the temperature was 25° on Election Day in the Pocono Mountains, but that didn't stop members of our team from showing up at the polls in the early morning darkness for the first of four scheduled three hour shifts.

Pocono Township, while divided into four voting precincts, used three locations in Tannersville for casting ballots. Mountain View Park served as Precinct #1, St. Paul Lutheran Church as Precinct #3, and Northampton Community College campus covered Precincts #2 and #4.

PFI planned to have representatives at each location from the start of voting at 7am until the polls closed at 7pm. We soon learned that CCPT had the same idea.

As one who was never comfortable being approached by campaigners at the polls, I chose not to assume the role of approaching others. Instead, I opted to be "coffee boy" for the day, driving from one polling station to another with fresh hot coffee for those braving the late autumn chill.

Another role I would play once the polls closed that evening would be "Municipal Election Watcher," which would allow me special access to the polling station after 7pm while election officials tallied the votes. My station would be at Northampton Community College observing Precinct #4. I'd be there with Judi, who would be keeping an eye on Precinct #2. Taylor would be at St. Paul Lutheran Church while Donald would be at Mountain View Park. The plan was for each of us to receive the certified vote totals after officials completed their tally and text those numbers to Judi, who would total the four precincts and get back to everyone with the news, good or bad.

The beauty of driving from one polling station to another throughout the day was that it allowed me to get a good sense from our team as to the general mood of voters. It also gave me a chance to see firsthand the behavior of the opposition as they tried hard to dissuade voters from approving the first class referendum.

Throughout the day, the general feeling of PFI team members was positive but there were signs that a good number of voters did not support the referendum. Most residents were pleasant when approached but there were those who would ignore our team members, walking past them while intentionally averting eye contact. There were also some voters who expressed outright anger at our efforts and their indignation was always met with a smile and a kind word by representatives of PFI. Never, during the course of twelve hours, was anyone on our team certain that we would see victory by day's end. We felt good, but we couldn't be sure.

CCPT stayed on their game; sticking to the time-dishonored but often successful strategy of fear, telling all who would listen, and even those who wouldn't, that taxes would increase should the referendum pass. A car-size banner draped across one of their parked vehicles, to be seen by all who entered the parking lot of one polling station, screamed, "VOTING YES MEANS HIGHER TAXES!" The opposition had no ammunition other than this tired scare tactic and they used it well, with no sense of shame.

Each polling station manned by PFI and CCPT sported their own easel-mounted sign highlighting the reasons for their stance. CCPT stuck to their usual message. While many residents knew better and were growing weary of the deceptive higher-tax campaign waged by the opposition, there were still a good number of undecided voters who could be influenced by the opposition's unrelenting assertions.

There were also those who would step into the voting booth completely confused on the issue. Enough so, that when all the votes were tallied later that night, there would prove to have been about fifty Pocono Township voters who choose not to cast a YES or NO vote for the first class referendum. Negative campaigning does work.

Disheartening as the opposition's campaign of misinformation and half-truths had been to PFI, the aggressiveness of those manning the polling stations for CCPT struck a raw nerve within our group. There were numerous reports of their representatives approaching our members while we were engaged in informative conversations with voters, countering what we were truthfully explaining. Others would stand in the parking lot and approach voters as they got out of their cars. Worse yet were the loud and repeated shouts to those entering the voting station, that a YES vote for first class is a YES vote for higher taxes. They were on a mission and, in essence, making their last stand. Nothing was sacred to them—except their hold on power.

Sixty-three cups of Dunkin' Donut coffee and four dozen donuts later, twelve hours after the darkness of the early morning saw the opening of the polls, 1548 residents of Pocono Township had cast their votes for or against first class. After ten months of hard work, dedication and steadfast determination, the moment of truth would soon be upon us.

There were six voting booths in the large meeting room at Northampton Community College, along with about a dozen voting officials. Three of the booths represented Precinct #2 and the other three, Precinct #4. Judi and I entered the room shortly before the doors were locked at exactly 7pm.

Well-organized officials immediately went about their job, looking as though they had gone through the routine many times before. Ballot boxes were removed from the voting booths, long rolls of paper were removed from the boxes and the booths were folded down for storage. What looked like long cash register receipts but held the vital voting tallies were lined up next to each other on a table as officials jotted down numbers from each. It wasn't long before results would be known.

Judi sat patiently in the back of the room as I paced, both of us nervously waiting for permission to view the tallies and see for ourselves the results. Precinct #2 finished first and Judi went over the numbers as I continued aimlessly walking back and forth.

Judi had her results before I even had a chance to view Precinct #4 tallies, and she looked relieved and satisfied as she approached me with the news. With a total of 344 votes in Precinct #2 the results showed 266 YES and 78 NO. We were certainly off to a great start.

With a more than three-to-one winning edge in Precinct #2, I naively expected to see the same margin when I would finally get to view the results of Precinct #4 a few minutes later. With 425 votes in #4, the winning margin was nowhere near that of #2 and I felt a slight emotional let-down as a result. Still it was a resounding victory with votes totaled at 244 YES and 181 NO.

Our optimism became a cautious confidence as Judi and I added together both sets of numbers while waiting to hear from

Taylor and Donald. Judi tried phoning each of them several times as we anxiously waited for their results.

Unexpectedly, a relaxed looking Taylor showed up outside our polling station with a smile on his face and announced his numbers. With 437 voters in Precinct #3, 245 voted YES and 192 voted NO. It was another impressive win for YES.

With the results of three out of four precincts in and the total votes standing at 755 YES to 451 NO, it now seemed impossible for the first class referendum to see defeat. Our confidence was building as we waited for the results from Donald and when he finally contacted us, our confidence turned to pure elation. With 302 voters in Precinct #1, first class was favored 183 to 119.

We did it! Our tallies showed a clear victory with a total of 938 YES and 570 NO. Official numbers released the next day, including write-in votes, showed 967 voters for first class and only 581 against.

Almost 63% of the voters approved the first class referendum!

CHAPTER 25

WE MADE LOCAL HISTORY

The voters of Pocono Township had their say and the message was very clear. They loudly proclaimed they no longer wanted the current form of government. It was a complete rejection of the status-quo. Voters wanted change!

Residents would now see new leadership that, by the very nature of first class, would be more transparent and more responsive to the needs of all, as opposed to only the influential few.

Future leaders would no longer be bogged down with day-to-day administrative duties. Instead, they would be legislators, focusing on making policy and planning for the future growth of the township. Because they would no longer be able to appoint themselves to paid township jobs, their motivation for serving would be altruistic. Furthermore, by commissioners not taking paychecks, additional financial resources would become available to hire necessary qualified professional services to address the complex needs of an ever-growing township.[49]

With a five member board of commissioners, there would now be five diverse perspectives, more sharing of responsibility and better representation for all citizens. With four-year terms for commissioners, five diverse perspectives, and the requirement that commissioners cannot be employed by the township we could now expect to see more informed, transparent and independent decision-making on behalf of Pocono Township residents.[50]

We made local history on Election Day, 2013. It was a proud moment for those who supported the initiative and a great day for all of Pocono Township.

---

[49] Pocono First Website: http://poconofirst.org/frequently-asked-questions/
[50] Pocono First Website: http://poconofirst.org/frequently-asked-questions/

The success of PFI should serve as an ever-lasting reminder that it is we the people who have the ultimate power, not those we elect to represent us. We must always remember that they are our representatives. They work for us, not the other way around. When they fail to properly represent us, when they ignore the will of the people and favor only themselves or their friends, it is our responsibility as citizens to hold them accountable and, when necessary, fight for change. PFI has proven without a shadow of a doubt that change is always within our reach when the people allow their voices to be heard.

Pocono Township was not unique in its difficulties. It's very likely there are other townships in Pennsylvania (in fact, other small towns throughout the country) that face similar challenges.

What was unique for our community was that a small group of residents took it upon themselves to offer the voters a voice that could make a difference. Working within the system, under focused leadership and against strong odds, we resolved to do the right thing, in the right way and at the right time. We researched options, set a goal, made a plan, pushed forward with hard-work, determination and diligence, and fought the power elite. We made our case with honesty and maintained our integrity throughout the entire process.

Our fellow residents watched in earnest and, placing their trust in us, voted for what we were convinced to be in the best interest of all Pocono Township residents. We know we have made the right decision and now it is time to move forward.

The hard work continues.

Pocono Township residents overwhelmingly approved the first class referendum, but that didn't mean PFI could now rest easy. The Monroe County Court of Common Pleas announced that they would be taking applications for the five commissioner positions through November 27th, would review the applications and interview finalists the following month, and would have their selections made by years end.

The Court also made it clear that *"neither the applicants, nor their supporters are allowed to contact any of the judges on a candidate's behalf."*[51]

PFI decided that, while contacting the judges directly was understandably not an option, it was important for us to communicate just what it was that residents wanted to see in their new governing board. Diane continued to encourage the writing of letters to the Pocono Record and the first of a number of post-election letters to the editor appeared on November 22nd.

Looks forward to a better Poc. Township
In Your Opinion—Pocono Record

The Pocono Township residents stated clearly, 967 to 581; they want to change their local government. They want elected officials to govern, not to be employees. They want the increased accountability that the shorter term of four years will afford. And, they want leaders who are more public-servant-minded than political operatives.

---

[51] Pierce, D., "Monroe County sitting judges to select Pocono Twp. Commissioners" Pocono Record (11/13/13) http://www.poconorecord.com/apps/pbcs.dll/article?AID=/20131113/NEWS/311130334

As part of the Pocono First Initiative group, I know firsthand how very well this diverse, grassroots group functioned. It worked hard and remained committed to the high ground; no mudslinging, no name-calling. However, no grassroots group, regardless how great, could ever convince voters to change from a certain to an uncertain form of government if they were satisfied with their current officials and township direction. So, while our focus has always been forward toward a better future, we were mindful of the things that troubled our township.

So, it is my hope that we will get five commissioners who will function well together, are not driven by party loyalty, conduct business in an open and fair manner, repeal unnecessary regulations, promote growth, find the most cost-effective ways to provide requisite services and make decisions that are in the best interest of the overall township. We are no different than any other community; we do not want our officials to be for sale. We want them to govern, ever mindful that they work for the residents, all the residents.

The court will do its job and I am confident it will do it well. It will, in earnest, look for those public servants who are best suited to move us forward. I look forward to supporting and volunteering to help our first-ever board of commissioners.[52]—**Judi Coover**

Letters would continue as we awaited the court's selection, most of them focusing on what qualities we would like to see in our future township leaders. It was our hope that the judges, as well as potential commissioner applicants, would read and take heed, so that the outcome of our yearlong effort would not be in vain.

My personal involvement with PFI began with the removal of Harold Werkheiser from his road master job. With the passage

---

[52]   Coover, J., "Looks forward to a better Poc. Township" In Your Opinion, Pocono Record (11/22/13) http://www.poconorecord.com/apps/pbcs.dll/article?AID=/20131122/NEWS04/311220334/-1/news0401

of our referendum and with the township soon to be under new leadership, the thought of his position being returned to him became a distinct possibility. I felt it was important to get the word out to those who would be our future commissioners, that rehiring Werkheiser would be proper. Doing so might even end the pending lawsuit against Pocono Township. With that in mind, I wrote the following:

Werkheiser can do the road job
In Your Opinion—Pocono Record

I've resided in Pocono Township for 26 years and if there's one thing I've said year after year, it's that our roads have always been well maintained.

When there was snow, there were plows. A pothole? Fixed before you knew it. I once saw a need for a sign to warn drivers of a dangerous turn in our road. The sign was there within a week. As long as money was allocated in the township budget for road work, it was done quickly and efficiently. These guys have always been great.

So, I'm one of many residents who believe that Harold Werkheiser was poorly treated when he was unceremoniously removed from his job as road master last January. He was a successful manager of a smooth-running road department. It would be nice to see him back in that job.

Harold handled this ill treatment with dignity. And his re-election campaign for supervisor, with style and grace. He knew that if First Class passed, he wouldn't have that supervisor job anyway. He didn't care. He wants what is best for the township. He's always wanted that.

It was a bittersweet victory for Harold on Election Day. What's great is that he knows a majority of our residents believe in him. That's got to make him feel good. But in the end, the First Class referendum did pass and there will no longer be supervisors.

Harold has a world of roadwork experience to offer Pocono Township. It is my hope and that of many other residents, that if there is to be a new road master, that he be chosen as the man for the job.

As we move forward as a first-class township, this would be not only a good thing to consider; it would be the right thing to do.[53]—**Jack Swersie**

Throughout the entire year, it was always my sincere hope that Werkheiser would eventually see the job of road master returned to him.

In a December 19th, 2013 Pocono Record article titled, "Pocono Twp., meet your newly appointed commissioners," David Pierce reported that the judges had made their decisions.

Pocono Twp., meet your newly appointed commissioners
By David Pierce—Pocono Record Writer

Six county judges named five men with a wide range of professional experience to oversee township operations. They are: Thomas E. Felver, Greg J. Hill, Gerald J. Lastowski, Richard P. Wielebinski and Bradley A. Wise.

Felver is a certified public accountant with Felver, Cefali & Associates. He served on the Cobble Creek Community Association Board for 10 years, including a term as the 160-home development's president. The 35-year township resident is a member and former president of the Tannersville Lions Club.

---

53   Swersie, J., "Werkheiser can do the road job" In Your Opinion, Pocono Record (12/12/13) http://www.poconorecord.com/apps/pbcs.dll/article?AID=/20131211/NEWS04/312110328/-1/news0401

Hill is a former business administrator for the city of Passaic, N.J. He has 33 years of municipal administration and management experience and has lived in the township for 16 years.

Lastowski taught social studies, history and economics at the Pocono Mountain School District for 35 years and was a coach. He is a 31-year township resident.

Wielebinski, a 10-county regional manager for Verizon, has been a ranger at Camelback Ski Resort for 15 years and a township resident for 23 years.

Wise, a former environmental engineer for PPL Electric Utilities, is a lifelong township resident and lifetime member of the Pocono Township Volunteer Fire Company.

More than 30 people applied for the five township commissioner openings.

The appointed commissioners will serve from Jan. 6, 2014, until Jan. 4, 2016.

Commissioner elections will take place in November 2015.[54]—**David Pierce**

Eight weeks into their two year terms as our interim commissioners, at the time this book was submitted for publication, the five new commissioners had already proven their commitment to excellence. The many challenges they faced were complex. The decisions they reached on behalf of our community were deliberate and executed with professionalism. Best of all, their focus was on only what was in the best interest of Pocono Township.

www.afirstclasstownship.com

---

[54] Pierce, D., "Pocono Twp., meet your newly appointed commissioners" Pocono Record (12/19/13) http://www.poconorecord.com/apps/pbcs.dll/article?AID=/20131219/NEWS/131219648